# The Virginia Housewife
## or, Methodical Cook

*a facsimile of an authentic
early American cookbook*

# Mary Randolph

*With a New Introduction by*
Janice Bluestein Longone

## DOVER PUBLICATIONS, INC.
### New York

## Copyright

## Bibliographical Note

This Dover edition, first published in 1993, is an unabridged, unaltered republication of the edition by E. H. Butler & Co., Philadelphia, 1860, under the title *The Virginia Housewife: Or Methodical Cook*, by "Mrs. Mary Randolph." The first edition had been published in Washington, 1824. Janice Bluestein Longone has written a new Introduction specially for the Dover edition.

## Library of Congress Cataloging-in-Publication Data

Randolph, Mary, 1762–1828.
    The Virginia housewife, or, Methodical cook : a facsimile of an authentic early American cookbook / Mary Randolph ; with a new introduction by Janice Bluestein Longone.
       p.    cm.
    Reprint. Originally published: Philadelphia : E. H. Butler, 1860.
    Includes bibliographical references.
    ISBN 0-486-27772-0
    1. Cookery—Virginia. I. Title. II. Title: Methodical cook.
TX715.R215 1993
641.59755—dc20
                                       93-32924
                                          CIP

Manufactured in the United States by Courier Corporation
27772008
www.doverpublications.com

# INTRODUCTION TO THE DOVER EDITION

AN AMERICAN CLASSIC. The first truly American cookbook. The first regional American cookbook. The first Southern cookbook. One of the most influential, one of the best cookbooks ever published in America. All of this praise has been lavished on Mary Randolph's *The Virginia House-Wife.*

Why? Is the praise justified? A simple perusal of the book, its recipes, its influence and the life of its author, together with an examination of the various commentaries on it, offers ample justification for our affirming that it is, indeed, special.

*The Virginia House-Wife* was first published in Washington, D.C., in 1824. Before then, very few cookbooks had been printed in America. The first, a reprint of a popular eighteenth-century English classic with very minor adaptation for the American colonial housewife, was E. Smith's *The Compleat Housewife,* published in Williamsburg in 1742. For the next half-century, reprints of English cookbooks continued to be published in the States. Then, in 1796 in Hartford, Connecticut, the first known cookbook of American authorship appeared, Amelia Simmons' *American Cookery.* For the next quarter-century, reprints of English classics continued to be published, such as those by E. Smith, Susannah Carter, Elizabeth Raffald, Richard Briggs, Hannah Glasse, Frederic Nutt, Mrs. Rundell and Dr. Kitchiner. During this same period, more than fifteen reprinted and/or pirated editions of Amelia Simmons' *American Cookery* as well as a small number of other minor cookery works by American authors were also published.

However, no important new cookbook of American authorship appeared until Mrs. Randolph published her *The Virginia House-Wife* in 1824. It was an immediate success and went through at least nineteen editions before the outbreak of the Civil War. In addition, copies appeared in the late nineteenth century and at least three modern reprints have been published, apart from the one in hand. Of the modern reprints, I can direct the attention of the reader to the fine historical notes and commentaries to be found in the edition edited by culinary historian Karen Hess and published by the

University of South Carolina Press in 1984. It contains an excellent analysis of the recipes and cooking methods. The edition published the same year by Oxmoor House/*Southern Living* as part of its Antique American Cookbook Series contains interesting biographical information on Mrs. Randolph.

With the appearance of this Dover edition, *The Virginia House-Wife* has been in and out of print for about 170 years. We may be most grateful to the editors of Dover Publications for once again making available, in a convenient and inexpensive format, an American cookery classic. Adding this edition to their already well-received facsimile of America's first cookbook, Amelia Simmons'.*American Cookery*, with its splendid introduction by Mary Tolford Wilson, Dover offers the historian a fine base upon which to build a library of culinary Americana.

The recipes in *The Virginia House-Wife* are simply splendid: "ochra" soup, catfish soup, barbecued "shote" ("This is the name given in the southern states to a fat young hog"); curry of catfish, "ochra" and tomatoes; gumbo ("A West India Dish"), chicken pudding ("A Favourite Virginia Dish"), field peas, "apoquiniminc" cakes (a form of beaten biscuits). Clearly we are in the South. For many of these recipes, this is their first printed appearance. But Mrs. Randolph knew about much more than Southern cooking; she includes recipes from England, France, Spain, the East Indies, the West Indies and New England ("Dough Nuts—A Yankee Cake"), among others. Her Spanish dishes are most intriguing: "gaspacho," "ropa veija," "ollo." We find polenta, vermicelli, macaroni and curry. We find recipes for corning, for "fricando" and fricassee, for haricot and matelote and salmagundi; we have "a-la-modes," "a-la-daubs" and "a-la-cremes." We learn how to "caveach" fish and to "pitchcock" eel. Mrs. Randolph tells us how to pickle several dozen items, including oysters, sturgeon, lemons, onions, nasturtiums, radish pods, English walnuts, peppers, green nectarines and asparagus.

Anyone who doubts that early Americans savored salads and vegetables need only look at what Mrs. Randolph offers. There are recipes for artichokes, asparagus, broccoli, cabbage, carrots, cauliflower, celery, cucumbers, eggplant, French beans, Jerusalem artichokes, lima beans, mushrooms, onions, parsnips, peas, peppers, potatoes, potato pumpkin, red beet roots, salsify, savoy cabbage, sea kale, sorrel, spinach, sprouts and young greens, squash, sweet potatoes, turnips, turnip tops, winter squash, onions and tomatoes. Indeed, Mrs. Randolph has seventeen recipes using tomatoes in the various editions of her cookbook. This provides further evidence to correct the misinformation that Americans did not use tomatoes prior to the mid-nineteenth century.

Mrs. Randolph made ample use of herbs, spices and flavorings. I note allspice, burnet, cayenne, celery seed, celery tops, chervil, cinnamon, cloves, coriander seed, cress, cumin seed, curry, garlic, ginger, green fennel, lavender, lemon, lemon peel, mace, marjoram, mint, mushroom powder, mustard, mustard seed, nutmeg, parsley, peppergrass, rosemary, rue, sage, savory, shallots, tansy, tarragon, thyme, turmeric, vanilla, wormwood, young fennel and young scallions, in addition to salt, pepper and a variety of catsups, including mushroom and walnut. She also flavored her dishes with anchovies, capers, horseradish, pickles, relishes, rose and orange waters, and vinegars. In addition, Mrs. Randolph freely, perhaps even extravagantly, used wines and spirits in her cooking.

Mention must be made of Mrs. Randolph's wondrous ice-cream recipes. There are twenty-two flavors, plus variations, including black walnut, pineapple, quince, peach, pear, chocolate, citron and almond.

Mary Randolph obviously had a fine palate and was a most sophisticated cook. But there is more to Mrs. Randolph than her recipes. There are hundreds of hints, admonitions, rules and bits of sage advice on cooking. In her section on ice creams, for example, she states, "It is the practice of some indolent cooks, to set the freezer containing the cream, in a tub with ice and salt, and put it in the ice house; it will certainly freeze there; but not until the watery particles have subsided, and by the separation destroyed the cream." She then offers a scientific discussion of how a proper ice cream should be made, and why each detailed step in the process is necessary.

Her recipe for asparagus on toast calls for cooking to what we would today call the *al dente* stage: "Great care must be taken to watch the exact time of their becoming tender; take them just at that instant, and they will have their true flavor and colour; a minute or two more boiling destroys both." She further suggests that the toast be lightly dipped in the liquor in which the asparagus was boiled, and "lay it in the middle of a dish; pour some melted butter on the toast, and lay the asparagus upon it; let it project beyond the asparagus, that the company may see there is a toast." Fifty years ago in New England, my mother often made this very dish for me, when I came home from school at lunchtime. As to peas, Mrs. Randolph says, "To have them in perfection, they must be quite young, gathered early in the morning, kept in a cool place, and not shelled until they are to be dressed." Still sage advice.

But there is yet more to Mrs. Randolph's prowess. The title page of her book bears the motto "Method is the Soul of Management." She didactically sets forth numerous rules for managing a household:

> The grand arcanum of management lies in three simple rules:—"Let every thing be done at the proper time, keep every thing in its proper place, and put every thing to its proper use."

> Management is an art that may be acquired by every woman of good sense and tolerable memory.

> Profusion is not elegance—a dinner justly calculated for the company, and consisting for the greater part of small articles, correctly prepared, and neatly served up, will make a much more pleasing appearance to the sight, and give a far greater gratification to the appetite, than a table loaded with food, and from the multiplicity of dishes, unavoidably neglected in the preparation, and served up cold.

In the Introduction (which does not appear in the first edition) Mrs. Randolph spells out in detail her underlying philosophy of house-keeping, a woman's duties and responsibilities, and household management:

> The prosperity and happiness of a family depend greatly on the order and regularity established in it. The husband, who can ask a friend to partake of his dinner in full confidence of finding his wife unruffled by the petty vexations attendant on the neglect of household duties—who can usher his guest into the dining room assured of seeing that methodical nicety which is the essence of true elegance,—will feel pride and exultation in the possession of a companion, who gives to his home charms that gratify every wish of his soul, and render the haunts of dissipation hateful to him. The sons bred in such a family will be moral men, of steady habits; and the daughters . . . will each be a treasure to her hus-band; and being formed on the model of an exemplary mother, will use the same means for securing the happiness of her own family. . . .

Mary Randolph came by her taste, intelligence and ability by dint of her birth and hard experience of life. Born to a wealthy and well-related Virginia family on August 9, 1762, she grew up at

Tuckahoe Plantation, there learning all about running a large Southern household. In 1782 she married a cousin, David Meade Randolph, thus further consolidating her relationship with the leading families of Virginia—the Lees, the Byrds, the Carters, the Carys, the Custises, Washingtons, and Jeffersons. Mary's ties to Thomas Jefferson were numerous and complex. Her brother married Jefferson's daughter Martha and her father had been brought up with Jefferson as foster brothers in the same Virginia household. However, her husband's and her own sharp political differences with Jefferson eventually led to scandal and impoverishment.

Prior to that, Mary and her husband first lived and entertained at their tobacco plantation on the James River, where Mary managed the household and its forty servants. They then moved to Richmond, where Mrs. Randolph gained great fame for her lavish hospitality at Moldavia, the mansion they built, named after Mary (who was always known as Molly) and her husband David.

In January 1808 impoverishment led Mrs. Randolph to open a boardinghouse to help feed her family. At that time, running a boardinghouse was one of the few occupations respectable enough for a woman of her social class to engage in. Her reputation for fine food guaranted the success of the endeavor.

About 1820, the Randolphs moved to Washington, D.C., and in 1824 Mary brought out *The Virginia House-Wife*. She died there on January 23, 1828 (the 1831 date of the Preface to the edition of that year was put there by someone else), and was buried at the Custis mansion in what was to become Arlington National Cemetery. Thus, given her relationship to the Custises, Mary Randolph was laid to rest on family ground.

The influence of Mary Randolph and *The Virginia House-Wife* cannot be overstated. Perhaps the most poignant tribute can be found in Susan Smedes's *Memorials of a Southern Planter* published in 1887. In praising her family butler, George Orris, she says, "It is only necessary to say to him that a certain number of guests were looked for to dinner, and everything would be done in a style to suit the occasion. George himself was said to know by heart every recipe in Mrs. Randolph's cookery-book, having been trained by that lady herself. Virginia tradition says that Mrs. Randolph had spent three fortunes in cooking."

JANICE (JAN) BLUESTEIN LONGONE

*The Wine and Food Library*
*Ann Arbor, Michigan*
*April 1993*

## SELECTED BIBLIOGRAPHY

Baron, Robert C. *The Garden and Farm Books of Thomas Jefferson.* Golden, Colorado: Fulcrum, 1987.

Hess, Karen. *Martha Washington's Booke of Cookery and Booke of Sweetmeats.* New York: Columbia University Press, 1981.

Husted, Margaret. "Mary Randolph's The Virginia Housewife." *Virginia Cavalcade* XXX, 2 (1980): 77-87. Richmond: The Virginia State Library.

Longone, Jan. "From the Kitchen: Tomatoes." *The American Magazine* 3 (No. 2, Autumn-Winter 1987-88): 54-60. Ann Arbor: The Clements Library, The University of Michigan.

Longone, Janice B. and Daniel T. *American Cookbooks and Wine Books.* Ann Arbor, Michigan: The Clements Library and The Wine and Food Library, 1984.

Lowenstein, Eleanor. *American Cookery Books 1742-1860.* Worcester, Massachusetts: American Antiquarian Society, 1972.

Randolph, Mary. *The Virginia Housewife.* With introduction by Shirley Abbott. Birmingham, Alabama: Oxmoor House, Inc., 1984.

_____ *The Virginia House-Wife.* With introduction by Karen Hess. South Carolina: University of South Carolina Press, 1984.

Simmons, Amelia. *American Cookery.* Hartford: Hudson & Goodwin, 1796. (Facsimile, with introduction by Mary Tolford Wilson, New York: Oxford University Press, 1958; and New York: Dover Publications, 1984.)

Smedes, Susan Dabney. *Memorials of a Southern Planter.* Baltimore: Cushings & Bailey, 1887.

THE

# VIRGINIA

# HOUSEWIFE:

OR

## METHODICAL COOK.

BY MRS. MARY RANDOLPH.

METHOD IS THE SOUL OF MANAGEMENT

PHILADELPHIA:

PUBLISHED BY E. H. BUTLER & CO.

1860

# PREFACE

THE difficulties I encountered when I first entered on the duties of a housekeeping life, from the want of books sufficiently clear and concise to impart knowledge to a Tyro, compelled me to study the subject, and by actual experiment to reduce every thing in the culinary line, to proper weights and measures. This method I found not only to diminish the necessary attention and labour, but to be also economical: for, when the ingredients employed were given in just proportions, the article made was always equally good. The government of a family, bears a Lilliputian resemblance to the government of a nation. The contents of the Treasury must be known, and great care taken to keep the expenditures from being equal to the receipts. A regular system must be introduced into each department, which may be modified until matured, and should then pass into an inviolable law. The grand arcanum of management lies in three simple rules:—"Let every thing be done at a proper time, keep every thing in its proper place, and put every thing to its proper use." If the mistress of a family, will every morning examine minutely the different departments of her household, she must detect errors in their infant state, when they can be corrected with ease; but a few days' growth gives them gigantic strength: and disorder, with all her attendant evils, are introduced. Early rising is also essential to the good government of a family. A late breakfast deranges the whole business of the day, and throws a portion of it on the next, which opens the door for confusion to enter. The greater part of the following receipts have been written from memory, where they were impressed by long continued practice. Should they prove serviceable to the young inexperienced housekeeper, it will add greatly to that gratification which an extensive circulation of the work will be likely to confer.

M. RANDOLPH.

*Washington, January,* 1831.

# INTRODUCTION

MANAGEMENT is an art that may be acquired by every woman of good sense and tolerable memory. If, unfortunately, she has been bred in a family where domestic business is the work of chance, she will have many difficulties to encounter; but a determined resolution to obtain this valuable knowledge, will enable her to surmount all obstacles. She must begin the day with an early breakfast, requiring each person to be in readiness to take their seats when the muffins, buckwheat cakes, &c. are placed on the table. This looks social and comfortable. When the family breakfast by detachments, the table remains a tedious time; the servants are kept from their morning's meal, and a complete derangement takes place in the whole business of the day. No work can be done till breakfast is finished. The Virginia ladies, who are proverbially good managers, employ themselves, while their servants are eating, in washing the cups, glasses, &c.; arranging the cruets, the mustard, salt-sellers, pickle vases, and all the apparatus for the dinner table. This occupies but a short time, and the lady has the satisfaction of knowing that they are in much better order than they would be if left to the servants. It also relieves her from the trouble of seeing the dinner table prepared, which should be done every day with the same scrupulous regard to exact neatness and method, as if a grand company was expected. When the servant is required to do this daily, he soon gets into the habit of doing it well; and his mistress having made arrangements for him in the morning, there is no fear of bustle and confusion in running after things that may be called for during the hour of dinner. When the kitchen breakfast is over, and the cook has put all things in their proper places, the mistress should go in to give her orders. Let all the articles intended for the dinner, pass in review before her: have the butter, sugar, flour, meal, lard, given out in proper quantities; the catsup, spice, wine, whatever may be wanted for each dish, measured to the cook. The mistress must tax her own memory with all this: we have no right to expect slaves or hired servants to be more attentive to our interest than we ourselves are: they will never recollect these little articles until they are going to use them; the mistress must then be called out, and thus have the horrible drudgery of keeping house all day, when one hour devoted to it in the morning, would release her from trouble until the next day. There is economy as well as comfort in a regular mode of doing business. When the mistress gives out every thing, there is no waste; but if temptation be thrown in the way of subordinates, not many will have power to resist it; besides, it is an immoral act to place them in a situation which we pray to be exempt from ourselves.

The prosperity and happiness of a family depend greatly on the order and regularity established in it. The husband, who can ask a friend to partake of his dinner in full confidence of finding his wife unruffled by the petty vexations attendant on the neglect of household duties—who can usher his guest into the dining-room assured of seeing that methodical nicety which is the essence of true elegance,—will feel pride and exultation in the possession of a companion, who gives to his home charms that gratify every wish of his soul, and render the haunts of dissipation hateful to him. The sons bred in such a family will be moral men, of steady habits; and the daughters, if the mother shall have performed the duties of a parent in the superintendence of their education, as faithfully as she has done those of a wife, will each be a treasure to her husband; and being formed on the model of an exemplary mother, will use the same means for securing the happiness of her own family, which she has seen successfully practised under the paternal roof.

# CONTENTS

## PORK.

## FISH.

## POULTRY, &c.

Page | Page

## CAKES.

## COLD CREAMS.

## PRESERVES.

## CORDIALS, &c.

## PICKLING.

THE

# VIRGINIA HOUSEWIFE:

OR,

## METHODICAL COOK.

---

## SOUPS

---

### ASPARAGUS SOUP.

TAKE four large bunches of asparagus, scrape it nicely, cut off one inch of the tops, and lay them in water, chop the stalks and put them on the fire with a piece of bacon, a large onion cut up, and pepper and salt; add two quarts of water, boil them till the stalks are quite soft, then pulp them through a sieve, and strain the water to it, which must be put back in the pot; put into it a chicken cut up, with the tops of asparagus which had been laid by, boil it until these last articles are sufficiently done, thicken with flour, butter and milk, and serve it up.

---

### BEEF SOUP.

TAKE the hind shin of beef, cut off all the flesh off the leg-bone, which must be taken away entirely, or the soup will be greasy. Wash the meat clean and lay it in a pot, sprinkle over it one small table-spoonful of pounded black pepper, and two of salt; three onions the size of a hen's egg, cut small, six small carrots scraped and cut up, two small turnips pared and cut into dice; pour on three quarts of water, cover the pot close, and keep it gently and steadily boiling five hours, which will leave about three pints of clear soup; do not let the pot boil over, but take off the scum carefully, as it rises. When it has boiled four hours, put in a small bundle of thyme and parsley, and a pint of celery cut small, or a tea-spoonful of celery seed pounded. These latter ingredients would lose their delicate flavour if boiled too much. Just before you take it up, brown it in the following manner: put a small table-spoonful of nice brown sugar into an iron skillet, set it on the fire and stir it till it melts and looks very dark, pour into it a ladle full of the soup, a little at a time; stirring it all the while. Strain this browning and mix it well with the soup; take out the bundle of thyme and parsley, put the nicest pieces of meat in your tureen, and pour on the soup and vegetables; put in some toasted bread cut in dice, and serve it up.

## GRAVY SOUP.

GET eight pounds of coarse lean beef—wash it clean and lay it in your pot, put in the same ingredients as for the shin soup, with the same quantity of water, and follow the process directed for that. Strain the soup through a sieve, and serve it up clear, with nothing more than toasted bread in it; two table-spoonsful of mushroom catsup will add a fine flavour to the soup

## SOUP WITH BOUILLI.

TAKE the nicest part of the thick brisket of beef, about eight pounds, put it into a pot with every thing directed for the other soup; make it exactly in the same way, only put it on an hour sooner, that you may have time to prepare the bouilli; after it has boiled five hours, take out the beef, cover up the soup and set it near the fire that it may keep hot. Take the skin off the beef, have the yelk of an egg well beaten, dip a feather in it and wash the top of your beef, sprinkle over it the crumb of stale bread finely grated, put it in a Dutch oven previously heated, put the top on with coals enough to brown, but not burn the beef; let it stand nearly an hour, and prepare your gravy thus:— Take a sufficient quantity of soup and the vegetables boiled in it; add to it a table-spoonful of red wine, and two of mushroom catsup, thicken with a little bit of butter and a little brown flour; make it very hot, pour it in your dish, and put the beef on it. Garnish it with green pickle, cut in thin slices, serve up the soup in a tureen with bits of toasted bread.

---

## VEAL SOUP.

PUT into a pot three quarts of water, three onions cut small, one spoonful of black pepper pounded, and two of salt, with two or three slices of lean ham; let it boil steadily two hours; skim it occasionally, then put into it a shin of veal, let it boil two hours longer; take out the slices of ham, and skim off the grease if any should rise, take a gill of good cream, mix with it two table-spoonsful of flour very nicely, and the yelks of two eggs beaten well, strain this mixture, and add some chopped parsley; pour some soup on by degrees, stir it well, and pour it into the pot, continuing to stir until it has boiled two or three minutes to take off the raw taste of the eggs. If the cream be not perfectly sweet, and the eggs quite new, the thickening will curdle in the soup. For a change you may put a dozen ripe tomatos in, first taking off their skins, by letting them stand a few minutes in hot water, when they may be easily peeled. When made in this way you must thicken it with the flour only. Any part of the veal may be used, but the shin or knuckle is the nicest.

## OYSTER SOUP.

Wash and drain two quarts of oysters, put them on with three quarts of water, three onions chopped up, two or three slices of lean ham, pepper and salt; boil it till reduced one-half, strain it through a sieve, return the liquid into the pot, put in one quart of fresh oysters, boil it till they are sufficiently done, and thicken the soup with four spoonsful of flour, two gills of rich cream, and the yelks of six new laid eggs beaten well; boil it a few minutes after the thickening is put in. Take care that it does not curdle, and that the flour is not in lumps; serve it up with the last oysters that were put in. If the flavour of thyme be agreeable, you may put in a little, but take care that it does not boil in it long enough to discolour the soup.

## BARLEY SOUP.

Put on three gills of barley, three quarts of water, few onions cut up, six carrots scraped and cut into dice, an equal quantity of turnips cut small; boil it gently two hours, then put in four or five pounds of the rack or neck of mutton, a few slices of lean ham, with pepper and salt; boil it slowly two hours longer and serve it up. Tomatos are an excellent addition to this soup.

## DRIED PEA SOUP.

Take one quart of split peas, or Lima beans, which are better; put them in three quarts of very soft water with three onions chopped up, pepper and salt; boil them two hours; mash them well and pass them through a sieve; return the liquid into the pot, thicken it with a large piece of butter and flour, put in some slices of nice salt pork, and a large tea-spoonful of celery seed pounded; boil it till the pork is done, and serve it up; have some toasted bread cut into dice and fried in butter, which must be put in the tureen before you pour in the soup.

## GREEN PEA SOUP.

Make it exactly as you do the dried pea soup, only in place of the celery seed, put a handful of mint chopped small, and a pint of young peas, which must be boiled in the soup till tender; thicken it with a quarter of a pound of butter, and two spoonsful of flour.

## OCHRA SOUP.

Get two double handsful of young ochra, wash and slice it thin, add two onions chopped fine, put it into a gallon of water at a very early hour in an earthen pipkin, or very nice iron pot; it must be kept steadily simmering, but not boiling: put in pepper and salt. At 12 o'clock, put in a handful of Lima beans; at

half-past one o'clock, add three young cimlins cleaned
and cut in small pieces, a fowl, or knuckle of veal, a
bit of bacon or pork that has been boiled, and six tomatos, with the skin taken off; when nearly done,
thicken with a spoonful of butter, mixed with one of
flour.    Have rice boiled to eat with it.

## HARE OR RABBIT SOUP.

Cut up two hares, put them into a pot with a piece
of bacon, two onions chopped, a bundle of thyme and
parsley, which must be  taken out before the soup is
thickened, add  pepper,  salt,  pounded  cloves,  and
mace, put in  a sufficient quantity of water, stew  it
gently three  hours, thicken with a large  spoonful of
butter, and one of brown flour, with a glass of red
wine; boil it a few  minutes longer, and serve it up
with the nicest parts of the hares.   Squirrels make
soup equally good, done the same way.

## SOUP OF ANY KIND OF OLD FOWL,
### *The only way in which  they are eatable.*

Put the fowls in a coop and feed them moderately
for a fortnight; kill one and cleanse it, cut off the
legs and wings, and separate the breast from the ribs,
which, together with the whole back, must be thrown
away, being too gross and strong for use.   Take the
skin and fat from the parts cut off which are also gross.
Wash the pieces nicely, and put them on the fire with
about a pound of bacon, a large onion chopped small,
some pepper and salt, a few blades of mace, a handful of parsley, cut up very fine, and two quarts of
water, if it be a common fowl or duck—a turkey will
require more water.   Boil it gently for three hours,

tie up a small bunch of thyme, and let it boil in it half an hour, then take it out. Thicken your soup with a large spoonful of butter rubbed into two of flour, the yelks of two eggs, and half a pint of milk. Be careful not to let it curdle in the soup.

## CATFISH SOUP,

*An excellent dish for those who have not imbibed a needless prejudice against those delicious fish.*

TAKE two large or four small white catfish that have been caught in deep water, cut off the heads, and skin and clean the bodies; cut each in three parts, put them in a pot, with a pound of lean bacon, a large onion cut up, a handful of parsley chopped small. some pepper and salt, pour in a sufficient quantity of water, and stew them till the fish are quite tender but not broken; beat the yelks of four fresh eggs add to them a large spoonful of butter, two of flour, and half a pint of rich milk; make all these warm and thicken the soup, take out the bacon, and put some of the fish in your tureen, pour in the soup, and serve it up.

## ONION SOUP.

CHOP up twelve large onions, boil them in three quarts of milk and water equally mixed, put in a bit of veal or fowl, and a piece of bacon with pepper and salt. When the onions are boiled to pulp, thicken it with a large spoonful of butter mixed with one of flour. Take out the meat, and serve it up with toasted bread cut in small pieces in the soup.

## TO DRESS TURTLE.

KILL it at night in winter, and in the morning in summer. Hang it up by the hind fins, cut off the head and let it bleed well. Separate the bottom shell from the top, with great care, lest the gall bladder be broken, which must be cautiously taken out and thrown away. Put the liver in a bowl of water. Empty the guts and lay them in water; if there be eggs, put them also in water. It is proper to have a separate bowl of water for each article. Cut all the flesh from the bottom shell, and lay it in water; then break the shell in two, put it in a pot after having washed it clean; pour on as much water as will cover it entirely, add one pound of middling, or flitch of bacon, with four onions chopped, and set it on the fire to boil. Open the guts, cleanse them perfectly; take off the inside skin, and put them in the pot with the shell; let them boil steadily for three hours, and if the water boils away too much, add more. Wash the top shell nicely after taking out the flesh, cover it, and set it by. Parboil the fins, clean them nicely—taking off all the black skin, and put them in water; cut the flesh taken from the bottom and top shell, in small pieces; cut the fins in two, lay them with the flesh in a dish; sprinkle some salt over, and cover them up. When the shell, &c. is done, take out the bacon, scrape the shell clean, and strain the liquor; about one quart of which must be put back in the pot; reserve the rest for soup; pick out the guts, and cut them in small pieces; take all the nice bits that were strained out, put them with the guts into the gravy; lay in the fins cut in pieces with them, and as much of the flesh as will be sufficient to fill the upper shell; add to it, (if a large turtle,) one bottle of white wine; cayenne pepper, and salt, to your taste, one gill of mushroom catsup, one gill of lemon pickle, mace, nutmegs and cloves, pounded, to season it high. Mix two large spoonsful of flour in one pound and a quarter of butter; put it in with thyme, parsley, marjoram and savory, tied in bunches; stew all these together, till the flesh and fins are tender; wash out the top shell, put a puff paste around the brim; sprinkle over the shell pepper and salt, then take the herbs out of the stew; if the gravy is not thick enough, add a little more flour, and fill the shell; should there be no eggs in the turtle, boil six new laid ones for ten minutes, put them in cold water a short time, peel them, cut them in two, and place them on the turtle; make a rich forcemeat, (see receipt for forcemeat,) fry the balls nicely, and put them also in the shell; set it in a dripping pan, with something under the sides to keep it steady; have the oven heated as for bread, and let it remain in it till nicely browned. Fry the liver and send it in hot.

## FOR THE SOUP.

At an early hour in the morning, put on eight pounds of coarse beef, some bacon, onions, sweet herbs, pepper and salt. Make a rich soup, strain it and thicken with a bit of butter, and brown flour; add to it the water left from boiling the bottom shell; season it very high with wine, catsup, spice and cayenne; put in the flesh you reserved, and if that is not enough, add the nicest parts of a well boiled calf's head; but do not use the eyes or tongue; let it boil till tender, and serve it up with fried forcemeat balls in it.

If you have curry powder, (see receipt for it,) it will give a higher flavour to both soup and turtle, than spice. Should you not want soup, the remaining flesh may be fried, and served with a rich gravy.

### MOCK TURTLE SOUP OF CALF'S HEAD.

HAVE a large head cleaned nicely without taking off the skin, divide the chop from the front of the head, take out the tongue, (which is best when salted,) put on the head with a gallon of water, the hock of a ham or a piece of nice pork, four or five onions, thyme, parsley, cloves and nutmeg, pepper and salt, boil all these together until the flesh on the head is quite tender, then take it up, cut all into small pieces, take the eyes out carefully, strain the water in which it was boiled, add half a pint of wine and a gill of mushroom catsup, let it boil slowly till reduced to two quarts, thicken it with two spoonsful of browned flour rubbed into four ounces of butter, put the meat in, and after stewing it a short time, serve it up. The eyes are a great delicacy.

# BEEF.

### DIRECTIONS FOR CURING BEEF.

PREPARE your brine in the middle of October, after the following manner: get a thirty gallon cask, take out one head, drive in the bung, and put some pitch on it, to prevent leaking. See that the cask is quite tight and clean. Put into it one pound of saltpetre powdered, fifteen quarts of salt, and fifteen gallons of cold water; stir it frequently, until dissolved, throw over the cask a thick cloth, to keep out the dust; look at it often and take off the scum. These proportions have been accurately ascertained—fifteen gallons of cold water will exactly hold, in solution, fifteen quaits of good clean Liverpool salt, and one pound of salt-petre: this brine will be strong enough to bear up an egg: if more salt be added, it will fall to the bottom without strengthening the brine, the water being already saturated. This brine will cure all the beef which a private family can use in the course of the winter, and requires nothing more to be done to it except occasionally skimming the dross that rises. It must be kept in a cool, dry place. For salting your beef, get a molasses hogshead and saw it in two, that the beef may have space to lie on; bore some holes in the bottom of these tubs, and raise them on one side about an inch, that the bloody brine may run off.

Be sure that your beef is newly killed—rub each piece very well with good Liverpool salt—a vast deal depends upon rubbing the salt into every part—it is unnecessary to put saltpetre on it; sprinkle a good deal of salt on the bottom of the tub. When the beef is well salted, lay it in the tub, and be sure you put the fleshy side downward. Put a great deal of salt on your beef after it is packed in the tub; this protects it from animals who might eat, if they could smell it, and does not waste the salt, for the beef can only dissolve a certain portion. You must let the beef lie in salt ten days, then take it out, brush off the salt, and wipe it with a damp cloth; put it in the brine with a bit of board and weight to keep it under.

In about ten days it will look red and be fit for the 'able, but it will be red much sooner when the brine becomes older. The best time to begin to salt beef is the latter end of October, if the weather be cool, and from that time have it in succession. When your beef is taken out of the tub, stir the salt about to dry, that it may be ready for the next pieces. Tongues are cured in the same manner.

## TO DRY BEEF FOR SUMMER USE.

The best pieces for this purpose are the thin briskets, or that part of the plate which is farthest from the shoulder of the animal, the round and rib pieces which are commonly used for roasting. These should not be cut with long ribs and the back-bones must be sawed off as close as possible, that the piece may lay flat in the dish. About the middle of February, select your beef from an animal well fatted with corn, and which, when killed, will weigh one hundred and fifty per quarter—larger oxen are always coarse. Salt the pieces as directed, let them lie one fortnight, then put them in brine, where they must remain three weeks: take them out at the end of the time, wipe them quite dry, rub them over with bran, and hang them in a cool, dry, and, if possible, dark place, that the flies may not get to them: they must be suspended, and not allowed to touch any thing. It will be necessary, in the course of the summer, to look them over occasionally, and after a long wet season, to lay them in the sun a few hours. Your tongues may be dried in the same manner: make a little hole in the root, run a twine through it, and suspend it. These dried meats must be put in a good quantity of water, to soak, the night before they are to be used. In boiling, it is absolutely necessary to have a large quantity of water to put the beef in while the water is cold, to boil steadily, skimming the pot, until the bones are ready to fall out; and, if a tongue, till the skin peels off with perfect ease: the skin must also be taken from the beef. The housekeeper who will buy good ox beef, and follow these directions exactly, may be assured of always having delicious beef on her table. Ancient prejudice has established a notion, that meat killed in the decrease of the moon, will draw up when cooked. The true cause of this shrinking, may be found in the old age of the animal, or in its diseased state, at the time of killing. The best age is from three to five years.

Few persons are aware of the injury they sustain, by eating the flesh of diseased animals. None but the Jewish butchers, who are paid exclusively for it, attend to this important circumstance. The best rule for judging that I have been able to discover, is the colour of the fat. When the fat of beef is a high shade of yellow, I reject it. If the fat of veal, mutton, lamb or pork, have the slightest tinge of yellow, I avoid it as diseased. The same rule holds good when applied to poultry.

## TO CORN BEEF IN HOT WEATHER.

TAKE a piece of thin brisket or plate, cut out the ribs nicely, rub it on both sides well with two large spoonsful of pounded saltpetre; pour on it a gill of molasses and a quart of salt; rub them both in; put it in a vessel just large enough to hold it, but not tight, for the bloody brine must run off as it makes, or the meat will spoil. Let it be well covered, top, bottom and sides, with the molasses and salt. In four days you may boil it, tied up in a cloth with the salt, &c. about it: when done, take the skin off nicely, and serve it up. If you have an ice-house or refrigerator, it will be best to keep it there. A fillet or breast of veal, and a leg or rack of mutton, are excellent done in the same way.

## IMPORTANT OBSERVATIONS ON ROAST-ING, BOILING, FRYING, &c.

In roasting butchers' meat, be careful not to run the spit through the nice parts: let the piece lie in water one hour, then wash it out, wipe it perfectly dry, and put it on the spit. Set it before a clear, steady fire: sprinkle some salt on it, and when it becomes hot, baste it for a time with salt and water: then put a good spoonful of nice lard into the dripping-pan, and when melted, continue to baste with it. When your meat, of whatever kind, has been down some time, but before it begins to look brown, cover it with paper and baste on it; when it is nearly done, take off the peper, dredge it with flour, turn the spit for some minutes very quick, and baste all the time to raise a froth—after which, serve it up. When mutton is roasted, after you take off the paper, loosen the skin and peel it off carefully, then dredge and froth it up Beef and mutton must not be roasted as much as veal, lamb, or pork; the two last must be skinned in the manner directed for mutton. You may pour a little melted butter in the dish with veal, but all the others must be served without sauce, and garnished with horse-radish, nicely scraped Be careful not to let a particle of dry flour be seen on the meat—it has a very ill appearance. Beef may look brown, but the whiter the other meats are, the more genteel are they, and if properly roasted, they may be perfectly done, and quite white. A loin of veal, and hind quarter of lamb, should be dished with the kidneys uppermost; and be sure to joint every thing that is to be separated at table, or it will be impossible to carve neatly. For those who *must* have gravy with these meats, let it be made in any way they like, and served in a boat. No meat can be well roasted except on a spit turned by a jack, and before a steady clear fire—other methods are no better than baking. Many cooks are in the habit of half boiling the meats to plump them as they term it, before they are spitted, but it destroys their fine flavour. Whatever is to be boiled, must be put into cold water with a little salt, which will cook them regularly. When they are put in boiling water, the outer side is done too much, before the inside gets heated. Nice lard is much better than butter for basting roasted meats, or for frying. To choose butchers' meat, you must see that the fat is not yellow, and that the lean parts are of a fine close grain, a lively colour, and will feel tender when pinched. Poultry should be well covered with white fat; if the bottom of the breast bone be gristly, it is young, but if it be a hard bone, it is an old one. Fish are judged by the liveliness of their eyes, and bright red of their gills. Dredge every thing with flour before it is put on to boil, and be sure to add salt to the water.

Fish, and all other articles for frying, after being nicely prepared, should be laid on a board and dredged with flour or meal mixed with salt: when it becomes dry on or,e side, turn it, and dredge the other. For broiling, have very clear coals, sprinkle a little salt and pepper over the pieces, and when done, dish them, and pour over some melted butter and chopped parsley—this is for broiled veal, wild fowl, birds or poultry: beef-steaks and mutton chops require only a table-spoonful of hot water to be poured over. Slice an onion in the dish before you put in the steaks or chops, and garnish both with rasped horse-radish. To have viands served in perfection, the dishes should be made hot, either by setting them over hot water, or by putting some in them, and the instant the meats are laid in and garnished, put on a. pewter dish cover. A dinner looks very enticing, when the steam rises from each dish on removing the covers, and if it be judiciously *ordered*, will have a double relish. Profusion is not elegance—a dinner justly calculated for the company, and consisting for the greater part of small articles, correctly prepared, and neatly served up, will make a much more pleasing appearance to the sight, and give a far greater gratification to the appetite, than a table loaded with food, and from the multiplicity of dishes, unavoidably neglected in the preparation, and served up cold.

There should always be a supply of brown flour kept in readiness to thicken brown gravies, which must be prepared in the following manner: put a pint of flour in a Dutch oven, with some coals under it: keep constantly stirring it until it is uniformly of a dark brown, but none of it burnt, which would look like dirt in the gravy. All kitchens should be provided with a saw for trimming meat, and also with larding needles.

## BEEF A-LA-MODE.

TAKE the bone from a round of beef, fill the space with a forcemeat made of the crumbs of a stale loaf, four ounces of marrow, two heads of garlic chopped with thyme and parsley, some nutmeg, cloves, pepper and salt, mix it to a paste with the yelks of four eggs beaten, stuff the lean part of the round with it, and make balls of the remainder; sew a fillet of strong linen wide enough to keep it round and compact, put it in a vessel just sufficiently large to hold it, add a pint of red wine, cover it with sheets of tin or iron, set it in a brick oven properly heated, and bake it three hours; when done, skim the fat from the gravy, thicken it with brown flour, add some mushroom and walnut catsup, and serve it up garnished with force-meat balls fried. It is still better when eaten cold with sallad.

## BRISKET OF BEEF BAKED.

BONE a brisket of beef, and make holes in it with a sharp knife about an inch apart, fill them alternately with fat bacon, parsley and oysters, all chopped small and seasoned with pounded cloves and nutmeg, pepper and salt, dredge it well with flour, lay it in a pan with a pint of red wine and a large spoonful of lemon pickle; bake it three hours, take the fat from the gravy and strain it; serve it up garnished with greer pickles.

## BEEF OLIVES.

CUT slices from a fat rump of beef six inches long and half an inch thick, beat them well with a pestle;

make a forcemeat of bread crumbs, fat bacon chopped, parsley, a little onion, some shred suet, pounded mace, pepper and salt; mix it up with the yelks of eggs, and spread a thin layer over each slice of beef, roll it up tight, and secure the rolls with skewers, set them before the fire, and turn them till they are a nice brown; have ready a pint of good gravy, thickened with brown flour and a spoonful of butter, a gill of red wine, with two spoonsful of mushroom catsup, lay the rolls in it, and stew them till tender; garnish with forcemeat balls.

## TO STEW A RUMP OF BEEF.

TAKE out as much of the bone as can be done with a saw, that it may lie flat on the dish, stuff it with forcemeat made as before directed, lay it in a pot with two quarts of water, a pint of red wine, some carrots and turnips cut in small pieces and stewed over it, a head of cellery cut up, a few cloves of garlic, some pounded cloves, pepper and salt, stew it gently till sufficiently done, skim the fat off, thicken the gravy, and serve it up; garnish with little bits of puff paste nicely baked, and scraped horse-radish.

## A FRICANDO OF BEEF.

CUT a few slices of beef six inches long, two or three wide, and one thick, lard them with bacon, dredge them well, and make them a nice brown before a brisk fire; stew them half an hour in a well seasoned gravy, put some stewed sorrel or spinage in the dish, lay on the beef, and pour over a sufficient quantity of gravy; garnish with fried balls.

## AN EXCELLENT METHOD OF DRESSING BEEF.

TAKE a rib roasting piece that has been hanging ten days or a fortnight, bone it neatly, rub some salt over t and roll it tight, binding it around with twine, put the spit through the inner fold without sticking it in the flesh, skewer it well and roast it nicely; when nearly done, dredge and froth it; garnish with scraped horse-radish.

## TO COLLAR A FLANK OF BEEF.

GET a nice flank of beef, rub it well with a large portion of saltpetre and common salt, let it remain ten days, then wash it clean, take off the outer and inner skin with the gristle, spread it on a board, and cover the inside with the following mixture: parsley, sage, thyme chopped fine, pepper, salt and pounded cloves; roll it up, sew a cloth over it, and bandage that with tape, boil it gently five or six hours, when cold, lay it on a board without undoing it, put another board on the top, with a heavy weight on it; let it remain twenty-four hours, take off the bandages, cut a thin slice from each end, serve it up garnished with green pickle and sprigs of parsley.

## TO MAKE HUNTERS' BEEF.

SELECT a fine fat round weighing about twenty-five pounds, take three ounces saltpetre, one ounce of cloves, half an ounce of alspice, a large nutmeg, and a quart of salt; pound them all together very fine, take the bone out, rub it well with this mixture on both sides, put some of it at the bottom of a tub just large enough to hold the beef, lay it in and strew the remainder on the top, rub it well every day for two weeks, and spread the mixture over it; at the end of this time, wash the beef, bind it with tape, to keep it round and compact, filling the hole where the bone was with a piece of fat, lay it in a pan of convenient size, strew a little suet over the top, and pour on it a pint of water, cover the pan with a coarse crust and a thick paper over that, it will take five hours baking; when cold take off the tape. It is a delicious relish at twelve o'clock, or for supper, eaten with vinegar, mustard, oil, or sallad. Skim the grease from the gravy and bottle it; it makes an excellent seasoning for any made dish.

## A NICE LITTLE DISH OF BEEF.

MINCE cold roast beef, fat and lean, very fine, add chopped onion, pepper, salt, and a little good gravy, fill scollop shells two parts full, and fill them up with potatos mashed smooth with cream, put a bit of butter on the top, and set them in an oven to brown.

## BEEF STEAKS.

THE best part of the beef for steaks, is the seventh and eighth ribs, the fat and lean are better mixed, and it is more tender than the rump if it be kept long enough; cut the steaks half an inch thick, beat them a little, have fine clear coals, rub the bars of the gridiron with a cloth dipped in lard before you put it over the coals, that none may drip to cause a bad smell, put no salt on till you dish them, broil them quick, turning them frequently; the dish must be very hot, put some slices of onion in it, lay in the steaks, sprinkle a little salt, and pour over them a spoonful of water and one of mushroom catsup, both made boiling hot, garnish with scraped horse-radish, and put on a hot dish cover. Every thing must be in readiness, for the great excellence of a beef steak lies in having it immediately from the gridiron.

## TO HASH BEEF.

Cut slices of raw beef, put them in a stew pan with a little water, some catsup, a clove of garlic, pepper and salt, stew them till done, thicken the gravy with a lump of butter rubbed into brown flour. A hash may be made of any kind of meat that has been cooked, but it is not so good, and it is necessary to have a gravy prepared and seasoned, and keep the hash over the fire only a few minutes to make it hot.

## BEEF STEAK PIE.

Cut nice steaks, and stew them till half done, put a puff paste in the dish, lay in the steaks with a few slices of boiled ham, season the gravy very high, pour it in the dish, put on a lid of paste and bake it.

## BEEF A-LA-DAUBE.

Get a round of beef, lard it well, and put it in a Dutch oven; cut the meat from a shin of beef, or any coarse piece in thin slices, put round the sides and over the top some slices of bacon, salt, pepper, onion, thyme, parsley, cellery tops, or seed pounded, and some carrots cut small, strew the pieces of beef over, cover it with water, let it stew very gently till per- fectly done, take out the round, strain the gravy, let it stand to be cold, take off the grease carefully, beat the whites of four eggs, mix a little water with them, put them to the gravy, let it boil till it looks clear, strain it, and when cold, put it over the beef.

# VEAL.

## DIRECTIONS FOR THE PIECES IN THE DIF- FERENT QUARTERS OF VEAL.

A LOIN of veal must always be roasted: the fillet or leg may be dressed in various ways, the knuckle or knee is proper for soup or for boiling; these are the pieces that compose the hind quarter. In the fore quarter, the breast and rack admit variety in cooking; the shoulder and neck are only fit for soup.

## VEAL CUTLETS FROM THE FILLET OR LEG.

CUT off the flank and take the bone out, then take slices the size of the fillet and half an inch thick, beat two yelks of eggs light, and have some grated bread mixed with pepper, salt, pounded nutmeg and chopped parsley; beat the slices a little, lay them on a board and wash the upper side with the egg, cover it thick with the bread crumbs, press them on with a knife, and let them stand to dry a little, that they may not fall off in frying, then turn them gently, put egg and crumbs on in the same manner, put them into a pan of boiling lard, and fry them a light brown; have some good gravy ready, season it with a tea-spoonful of curry powder, a large one of wine, and one of lemon pickle, thicken with butter and brown flour, drain every drop of lard from the cutlets, lay them in the gravy, and stew them fifteen or twenty minutes, serve them up garnished with lemon cut in thin slices

## VEAL CHOPS.

TAKE the best end of a rack of veal, cut it in chops, with one bone in each, leave the small end of the bone bare two inches, beat them flat, and prepare them with eggs and crumbs, as the cutlets, butter some half-sheets of white paper, wrap one round each chop, skewer it well, leaving the bare bone out, broil them till done, and take care the paper does not burn; have nice white sauce in a boat.

## VEAL CUTLETS.

CUT them from the fillet, put them in a stew pan with a piece of nice pork, a clove of garlic, a bundle of thyme and parsley, pepper and salt, cover them with water and let them stew ten or fifteen minutes, lay them on a dish, and when cold cover them well with the crumb of stale bread finely grated, mixed with the leaves of parsley chopped very small, some pepper, salt and grated nutmeg; press these on the veal with a knife, and when a little dried, turn it and do the same to the other side; put a good quantity of lard in a pan, when it boils lay the cutlets in carefully that the crumbs may not fall; fry them a little brown, lay them on a strainer to drain off the grease, do the same with the crumbs that have fallen in the pan: while this is doing, simmer the water they were boiled in to half a pint, strain it and thicken with four ounces of butter and a little browned flour; add a gill of wine and one of mushroom catsup, put in the cutlets and crumbs, and stew till tender; add forcemeat balls

## KNUCKLE OF VEAL.

Boil a half pint of pearl barley in salt and water till quite tender, drain the water from it and stir in a piece of butter, put it in a deep dish; have the knuckle nicely boiled in milk and water, and lay it on the barley, pour some parsley and butter over it.

## BAKED FILLET OF VEAL.

Take the bone out of the fillet, wrap the flap around and sew it, make a forcemeat of bread crumbs, the fat of bacon, a little onion chopped, parsley, pepper, salt, and a nutmeg pounded, wet it with the yelks of eggs, fill the place from which the bone was taken, make holes around it with a knife and fill them also, and lard the top; put it in a Dutch oven with a pint of water, bake it sufficiently, thicken the gravy with butter and brown flour, add a gill of wine and one of mushroom catsup, and serve it garnished with forcemeat balls fried.

## SCOTCH COLLOPS OF VEAL.

They may be made of the nice part of the rack, or cut from the fillet, rub a little salt and pepper on them, and fry them a light brown; have a rich gravy seasoned with wine, and any kind of catsup you choose, with a few cloves of garlic, and some pounded mace, thicken it. put the collops in and stew them a short time, take them out, strain the gravy over, and garnish with bunches of parsley fried crisp, and thin slices of middling of bacon, curled around a skewer and boiled

## VEAL OLIVES.

TAKE the bone out of the fillet and cut thin slices the size of the leg, beat them flat, rub them with the yelk of an egg beaten, lay on each piece a thin slice of boiled ham, sprinkle salt, pepper, grated nutmeg, chopped parsley, and bread crumbs over all, roll them up tight, and secure them with skewers, rub them with egg and roll them in bread crumbs, lay them on a tin dripping pan, and set them in an oven; when brown on one side, turn them, and when sufficiently done, lay them in a rich highly seasoned gravy made of proper thickness, stew them till tender, garnish with forcemeat balls and green pickles sliced.

## RAGOUT OF A BREAST OF VEAL.

SEPARATE the joints of the brisket, and saw off the sharp ends of the ribs, trim it neatly, and half roast it; put it in a stew pan with a quart of good gravy seasoned with wine, walnut and mushroom catsup, a tea-spoonful of curry powder, and a few cloves of garlic; stew it till tender, thicken the gravy, and garnish with sweatbreads nicely broiled.

## FRICANDO OF VEAL.

CUT slices from the fillet an inch thick and six inches long, lard them with slips of lean middling of bacon, bake them a light brown, stew them in well seasoned gravy, made as thick as rich cream, serve them up hot, and lay round the dish sorrel stewed with butter, pepper and salt, till quite dry.

## TO MAKE A PIE OF SWEETBREADS AND OYSTERS.

Boil the sweetbreads tender, stew the oysters, season them with pepper and salt, and thicken with cream, butter, the yelks of eggs and flour, put a puff paste at the bottom and around the sides of a deep dish, take the oysters up with an egg spoon, lay them in the bottom, and cover them with the sweetbreads, fill the dish with gravy, put a paste on the top, and bake it. This is the most delicate pie that can be made. The sweetbread of veal is the most delicious part, and may be broiled, fried, or dressed in any way, and is always good.

## MOCK TURTLE OF CALF'S HEAD.

Have the head nicely cleaned, divide the chop from the skull, take out the brains and tongue, and boil the other parts till tender, take them out of the water and put into it a knuckle of veal or four pounds of lean beef, three onions chopped, thyme, parsley, a tea-spoonful of pounded cloves, the same of mace, salt, and cayenne pepper to your taste—boil these things together till reduced to a pint, strain it, and add two gills of red wine, one of mushroom and one of walnut catsup, thicken it with butter and brown flour; the head must be cut in small pieces and stewed a few minutes in the gravy; put a paste round the edge of a deep dish, three folds, one on the other, but none on the bottom; pour in the meat and gravy, and bake it till the paste is done; pick all strings from the brains, pound them, and add grated bread, pepper and salt, make them in little cakes with the yelk of an egg, fry them a nice brown, boil six eggs hard, leave one whole and divide the others exactly in two, have some bits of paste nicely baked; when the head is taken from the oven, lay the whole egg in the middle, and dispose the others, with the brain cakes and bits of paste tastily around it. If it be wanted as soup, do not reduce the gravy so much, and after stewing the head, serve it in a tureen with the brain cakes and forcemeat balls fried, in place of the eggs and paste. The tongue should be salted and put in brine; they are very delicate, and four of them boiled and pealed, and served with four small chickens boiled, make a handsome dish, either cold or hot, with parsley and butter poured over them.

## TO GRILL A CALF'S HEAD.

CLEAN and divide it as for the turtle, take out the brains and tongue, boil it tender, take the eyes out whole, and cut the flesh from the skull in small pieces; take some of the water it was boiled in for gravy, put to it salt, cayenne pepper, a grated nutmeg, with a spoonful of lemon pickle; stew it till it is well flavoured, take the jowl or chop, take out the bones, and cover it with bread crumbs, chopped parsley, pepper and salt, set it in an oven to brown, thicken the gravy with the yelks of two eggs and a spoonful of butter rubbed into two of flour, stew the head in it a few minutes, put it in the dish, and lay the grilled chop on it; garnish it with brain cakes and broiled sweetbreads.

## TO COLLAR A CALF'S HEAD.

AFTER cleaning it nicely, saw the bone down the middle of the skull, but do not separate the head, take out the brains and tongue, boil it tender enough to remove the bones, which must be taken entirely out; lay it on a board, have a good quantity of chopped parsley seasoned with mace, nutmeg, pepper and salt—spread a layer of this, then one of thick slices of ham, another of parsley and one of ham, roll it up tight, sew a cloth over it, and bind that round with tape; boil it half an hour, and when cold press it. It must be kept covered with vinegar and water, and is very delicious eaten with sallad or oil and vinegar.

## CALF'S HEART, A NICE DISH.

TAKE the heart and liver from the harslet, and cut off the windpipe, boil the lights very tender, and cut them in small pieces—take as much of the water they were boiled in as will be sufficient for gravy; add to it a large spoonful of white wine, one of lemon pickle, some grated nutmeg, pepper and salt, with a large spoonful of butter, mixed with one of white flour; let it boil a few minutes, and put in the minced lights, set it by till the heart and liver are ready, cut the ventricle out of the heart, wash it well, lard it all over with narrow slips of middling, fill the cavity with good forcemeat, put it in a pan on the broad end, that the stuffing may not come out; bake it a nice brown, slice the liver an inch thick and broil it, make the mince hot, set the heart upright in the middle of the dish, pour it around, lay the broiled liver on, and garnish with bunches of fried parsley; it should be served up extremely hot.

## CALF'S FEET FRICASSEE.

Boil the feet till very tender, cut them in two and pull out the large bones, have half a pint of good white gravy, add to it a spoonful of white wine, one of lemon pickle, and some salt, with a tea-spoonful of curry powder, stew the feet in it fifteen minutes, and thicken it with the yelks of two eggs, a gill of milk, a large spoonful of butter, and two of white flour, let the thickening be very smooth, shake the stew pan over the fire a few minutes, but do not let it boil lest the eggs and milk should curdle.

## TO FRY CALF'S FEET.

Prepare them as for the fricassee, dredge them well with flour and fry them a light brown, pour parsley and butter over, and garnish with fried parsley.

## TO PREPARE RENNET.

Take the stomach from the calf as soon as it is killed—do not wash it, but hang it in a dry cool place for four or five days; then turn it inside out, slip off all the curd nicely with the hand, fill it with a little salt-petre mixed with the quantity of salt necessary, and lay it in a small stone pot, pour over it a small tea-spoonful of vinegar, and sprinkle a handful of salt over it, cover it closely and keep it for use. You must not wash it—that would weaken the gastric juice, and injure the rennet. After it has been salted six or eight weeks, cut off a piece four or five inches long, put it in a large mustard bottle, or any vessel that will hold about a pint and a half; put on it five gills of cold water, and two gills of rose brandy—stop it very close, and shake it when you are going to use it: a table-spoonful of this is sufficient for a quart of milk. It must be prepared in very cool weather, and if well done, will keep more than a year.

## TO HASH A CALF'S HEAD.

Boil the head till the meat is almost enough for eating; then cut it in thin slices, take three quarters of a pint of good gravy, and add half a pint of white wine, half a nutmeg, two anchovies, a small onion stuck with cloves, and a little mace; boil these up in the liquor for a quarter of an hour, then strain it and boil it up again; put in the meat, with salt to your taste, let it stew a little, and if you choose it, you may add some sweetbreads, and make some forcemeat balls with veal; mix the brains with the yelks of eggs and fry them to lay for a garnish. When the head is ready to be sent in, stir in a bit of butter.

## TO BAKE A CALF'S HEAD.

Divide the calf's head, wash it clean, and having the yelks of two eggs well beaten, wash the outside of the head all over with them, and on that strew raspings of bread sifted, pepper, salt, nutmeg and mace powdered; also, the brains cut in pieces and dipped in thick butter, then cover the head with bits of butter, pour into the pan some white wine and water, with as much gravy, and cover it close. Let it be baked in a quick oven, and when it is served up, pour on some strong gravy, and garnish with slices of lemon, red beet root pickled, fried oysters and fried bread.

---

## TO STUFF AND ROAST A CALF'S LIVER.

Take a fresh calf's liver, and having made a hole in it with a large knife run in lengthways, but not quite through, have ready a forced meat, or stuffing made of part of the liver parboiled, fat of bacon minced very fine, and sweet herbs powdered; add to these some grated bread and spice finely powdered, with pepper and salt. With this stuffing fill the hole in the liver, which must be larded with fat bacon, and then roasted, flouring it well, and basting with butter till it is enough. This is to be served up hot, with gravy sauce having a little wine in it.

---

## TO BROIL CALF'S LIVER.

Cut it in slices, put over it salt and pepper; broil it nicely, and pour on some melted butter with chopped parsley after it is dished.

---

*Directions for cleaning Calf's Head and Feet, for those who live in the country and butcher their own meats.*

As soon as the animal is killed, have the head and feet taken off, wash them clean, sprinkle some pounded rosin all over the hairs, then dip them in boiling water, take them instantly out, the rosin will dry immediately, and they may be scraped clean with ease; the feet should be soaked in water three or four days, changing it daily; this will make them very white

# LAMB.

### TO ROAST THE FORE-QUARTER, &c.

THE fore-quarter should always be roasted and served with mint sauce in a boat; chop the mint small and mix it with vinegar enough to make it liquid, sweeten it with sugar.

The hind-quarter may be boiled or roasted, and requires mint sauce; it may also be dressed in various ways.

### BAKED LAMB.

CUT the shank bone from a hind-quarter, separate the joints of the loin, lay it in a pan with the kidney uppermost, sprinkle some pepper and salt, add a few cloves of garlic, a pint of water and a dozen large ripe tomatos with the skins taken off, bake it but do not let it be burnt, thicken the gravy with a little butter and brown flour.

### FRIED LAMB.

SEPARATE the leg from the loin, cut off the shank and boil the leg; divide the loin in chops, dredge and fry them a nice brown, lay the leg in the middle of the dish, and put the chops around, pour over parsley and butter, and garnish with fried parsley.

The leg cut into steaks and the loin into chops will make a fine fricassee, or cutlets.

### TO DRESS LAMB'S HEAD AND FEET.

CLEAN them very nicely, and boil them till tender, take off the flesh from the head with the eyes, also

mince the tongue and heart, which must be boiled
with the head; split the feet in two, put them with
the pieces from the head and the mince, into a pint
of good gravy, seasoned with pepper, salt, and tomato
catsup, or ripe tomatos: stew it till tender, thicken
the gravy, and lay the liver cut in slices and broiled
over it—garnish with crisp parsley and bits of curled
bacon.

# MUTTON.

THE saddle should always be roasted and garnished
with scraped horse-radish. See general observations
on roasting. Mutton is in the highest perfection from
August until Christmas, when it begins to decline in
goodness.

## BOILED LEG OF MUTTON.

CUT off the shank, wrap the flank nicely round and
secure it with skewers, dredge it well with flour, and
put it on the fire in a kettle of cold water with some
salt, and three or four heads of garlic, which will give
it a delicately fine flavour; skin it well, and when
nearly done, take it from the fire and keep it hot and
closely covered, that the steam may finish it; have
carrots well boiled to put in the dish under it, or turnips boiled, mashed smooth and stewed with a lump
of butter and salt, lay the mutton on, and pour over
t butter melted with some flour in it, and a cup full
of capers with some of the vinegar; shake them
together over the fire till hot before you pour it on.

## ROASTED LEG.

PREPARE it as for boiling, be very careful in spit-ting it, cover it with paper and follow the directions for roasting, serve it up garnished with scraped horse-radish.

---

## BAKED LEG OF MUTTON.

TAKE the flank off, but leave all the fat, cut out the bone, stuff the place with a rich forcemeat, lard the top and sides with bacon, put it in a pan with a pint of water, some chopped onion and cellery cut small, a gill of red wine, one of mushroom catsup and a tea-spoonful of curry powder, bake it and serve it up with the gravy, garnish with forcemeat balls fried.

---

## STEAKS OF A LEG OF MUTTON.

CUT off the flank, take out the bone, and cut it in large slices half an inch thick, sprinkle some salt and pepper, and broil it, pour over it nice melted butter with capers; a leg cut in the same way and dressed as directed for veal cutlets, is very fine. It is also ex-cellent when salted as beef, and boiled, served up with carrots or turnips.

A shoulder of mutton is best when roasted, but may be made into cutlets or in a harrico.

---

## TO HARRICO MUTTON.

TAKE the nicest part of the rack, divide it into chops, with one bone in each, beat them flat, sprinkle salt and pepper on them, and broil them nicely; make a rich gravy out of the inferior parts, season it well with pepper, a little spice, and any kind of catsup you

choose; when sufficiently done, strain it, and thicken
it with butter and brown flour, have some carrots and
turnips cut into small dice and boiled till tender, put
them in the gravy, lay the chops in and stew them
fifteen minutes; serve them up garnished with green
pickle.

## MUTTON CHOPS.

Cut the rack as for the harrico, broil them, and
when dished, pour over them a gravy made with two
large spoonsful of boiling water, one of mushroom
catsup, a small spoonful of butter and some salt, stir it
till the butter is melted, and garnish with horse-radish
scraped.

## BOILED BREAST OF MUTTON.

Separate the joints of the brisket, and saw off the
sharp ends of the ribs, dredge it with flour, and boil
it; serve it up covered with onions—see onion sauce.

## BREAST OF MUTTON IN RAGOUT.

Prepare the breast as for boiling, brown it nicely
in the oven, have a rich gravy well seasoned and
thickened with brown flour, stew the mutton in it till
sufficiently done, and garnish with forcemeat balls
fried.

## TO GRILL A BREAST OF MUTTON

Prepare it as before, score the top, wash it over
with the yelk of an egg, sprinkle some salt, and
cover it with bread crumbs, bake it, and pour caper
sauce in the dish. It may also be roasted, the skin

taken off and frothed nicely, serve it up with good gravy, and garnish with current jelly cut in slices.

The neck of mutton is fit only for soup, the liver is very good when broiled.

## BOILED SHOULDER OF MUTTON.

Put it in cold water with some salt, and boil it till tender; serve it up covered with onion sauce.

## SHOULDER OF MUTTON WITH CELLERY SAUCE.

Wash and clean ten heads of cellery, cut off the green tops and take off the outside stalks, cut the heads in thin slices, boil them tender in a little milk, just enough for gravy, add salt, and thicken it with a spoonful of butter and some white flour; boil the shoulder and pour the sauce over it.

## ROASTED LOIN OF MUTTON.

Cut the loin in four pieces, take off the skin, rub each piece with salt, wash them with the yelk of an egg, and cover them thickly with bread crumbs, chopped parsley, pepper and salt; wrap them up securely in paper, put them on a bird spit, and roast them; put a little brown gravy in the dish, and garnish with pickle.

# PORK.

## TO CURE BACON.

Hogs are in the highest perfection, from two and a half to four years old, and make the best bacon, when

they do not weigh more than one hundred and fifty
or sixty at farthest; they should be fed with corn, six
weeks at least, before they are killed, and the shorter
distance they are driven to market, the better will
their flesh be.   To secure them against the possibility
of spoiling, salt them before they get cold; take out
the chine or back-bone from the neck to the tail, cut
the hams, shoulders and middlings; take the ribs from
the shoulders and the leaf fat from the hams: have
such tubs as are directed for beef, rub a large table
spoonful of saltpetre on the inside of each ham, for
some minutes, then rub both sides well with salt,
sprinkle the bottom of the tub with salt, lay the hams
with the skin downward, and put a good deal of salt
between each layer; salt the shoulders and middlings
in the same manner, but less saltpetre is necessary;
cut the jowl or chop from the head, and rub it with
salt and saltpetre.   You should cut off the feet just
above the knee joint; take off the ears and nose, and
lay them in a large tub of cold water for souse.   When
the jowls have been in salt two weeks, hang them up
to smoke—do so with the shoulders and middlings
at the end of three weeks, and the hams at the end
of four.   If they remain longer in salt they will be
hard.   Remember to hang the hams and shoulders
with the hocks down, to preserve the juices.   Make a
good smoke every morning, and be careful not to have
a blaze; the smoke-house should stand alone, for any
additional heat will spoil the meat.   During the hot
weather, beginning the first of April, it should be occasionally taken down, examined—rubbed with hick-
ory ashes, and hung up again.

The generally received opinion that saltpetre hard
ens meat, is entirely erroneous:—it tends greatly to
prevent putrefaction, but will not make it hard; neither
will laying in brine five or six weeks in cold weather,
have that effect, but remaining in salt too long, will
certainly draw off the juices, and harden it. Bacon
should be boiled in a large quantity of water, and a
ham is not done sufficiently, till the bone on the under
part comes off with ease. New bacon requires much
longer boiling than that which is old.

## TO MAKE SOUSE.

LET all the pieces you intend to souse, remain
covered with cold water twelve hours; then wash them
out, wipe off the blood, and put them again in fresh
water; soak them in this manner, changing the water
frequently, and keeping it in a cool place, till the
blood is drawn away; scrape and clean each piece
perfectly nice, mix some meal with water, add salt to
it, and boil your souse gently, until you can run a
straw into the skin with ease. Do not put too much
in the pot, for it will boil to pieces and spoil the
appearance. The best way is to boil the feet in one
pot, the ears and nose in another, and the heads in a
third; these should be boiled till you can take all the
bones out; let them get cold, season the insides with
pepper, salt, and a little nutmeg; make it in a tight
roll, sew it up close in a cloth, and press it lightly.
Mix some more meal and cold water, just enough to
look white; add salt, and one-fourth of vinegar; put
your souse in different pots, and keep it well covered
with this mixture, and closely stopped. It will be
necessary to renew this liquor every two or three

weeks. Let your souse get quite cold after boiling, before you put it in the liquor, and be sure to use pale coloured vinegar, or the souse will be dark. Some cooks singe the hair from the feet, *etcetera*, but this destroys the colour: good souse will always be white.

## TO ROAST A PIG.

THE pig must be very fat, nicely cleaned, and not too large to lie in the dish; chop the liver fine and mix it with crumbs of bread, chopped onion and parsley, with pepper and salt, make it into a paste with butter and an egg, stuff the body well with it, and sew it up, spit it, and have a clear fire to roast it; baste with salt and water at first, then rub it frequently with a lump of lard wrapped in a piece of clean linen; this will make it much more crisp than basting it from the dripping pan. When the pig is done, take off the head, separate the face from the chop, cut both in two and take off the ears, take out the stuffing, split the pig in two parts lengthways, lay it in the dish with the head, ears, and feet, which have been cut off, placed on each side, put the stuffing in a bowl with a glass of wine, and as much dripping as will make it sufficiently liquid, put some of it under the pig, and serve the rest in a boat.

## TO BARBECUE SHOTE.*

THIS is the name given in the southern states to a fat young hog, which, when the head and feet are

---

* Shote being a Provincial term, and not a legitimate English word, Mrs. R. has taken the liberty of spelling it in a way that conveys the sound of the pronunciation more clearly than *shoat*, the usual manner of spelling it.

taken off, and it is cut into four quarters, will weigh six pounds per quarter. Take a fore-quarter, make several incisions between the ribs, and stuff it with rich forcemeat; put it in a pan with a pint of water, two cloves of garlic, pepper, salt, two gills of red wine, and two of mushroom catsup, bake it, and thicken the gravy with butter and brown flour; it must be jointed, and the ribs cut across before it is cooked, or it cannot be carved well; lay it in the dish with the ribs uppermost; if it be not sufficiently brown, add a little burnt sugar to the gravy, garnish with balls.

## TO ROAST A FORE-QUARTER OF SHOTE.

JOINT it for the convenience of carving, roast it before a brisk fire; when done, take the skin off, dredge and froth it, put a little melted butter with some caper vinegar over it, or serve it with mint sauce.

## TO MAKE SHOTE CUTLETS.

TAKE the skin from the hind-quarter, and cut it in pieces, prepare them in the way directed for veal cutlets, make a little nice gravy with the skin and the scraps of meat left, thicken it with butter and brown flour, and season it in any way you like.

## TO CORN SHOTE.

RUB a hind-quarter with saltpetre and common salt, let it lie ten days, then boil it, and put either carrots or parsnips under it.

## SHOTE'S HEAD.

TAKE out the brains, and boil the head till quite tender, cut the heart and liver from the harslet, and boil the feet with the head; cut all the meat from the head in small pieces, mince the tongue and chop the brains small, take some of the water the head was boiled in, season it with onion, parsley and thyme, all chopped fine, add any kind of catsup—thicken it with butter and brown flour, stew the whole in it fifteen minutes, and put it in the dish: have the heart roasted to put in the middle, lay the broiled liver around, and garnish it with green pickle.

## LEG OF PORK WITH PEASE PUDDING.

BOIL a small leg of pork that has been sufficiently salted, score the top and serve it up; the pudding must be in a separate dish; get small delicate pease, wash them well, and tie them in a cloth, allowing a little room for swelling, boil them with the pork, then mash and season them, tie them up again and finish boiling it; take care not to break the pudding in turn ing it out.

## STEWED CHINE.

TAKE the neck chine, rub it well with salt, lay it in a pan, put it in a pint of water, and fill it up with sweet potatos nicely washed, but not peeled, cover it close and bake it till done; serve it up with the potatos, put a little of the gravy in the dish.

## TO TOAST A HAM.

BOIL it well, take off the skin, and cover the top thickly with bread crumbs, put it in an oven to brown, and serve it up.

## TO STUFF A HAM.

TAKE a well smoked ham, wash it very clean, make incisions all over the top two inches deep, stuff them quite full with parsley chopped small and some pepper, boil the ham sufficiently; do not take off the skin. It must be eaten cold.

## SOUSED FEET IN RAGOUT.

SPLIT the feet in two, dredge them with flour and fry them a nice brown; have some well seasoned gravy thickened with brown flour and butter; stew the feet in it a few minutes.

## TO MAKE SAUSAGES.

TAKE the tender pieces of fresh pork, chop them exceedingly fine—chop some of the leaf fat, and put them together in the proportion of three pounds of pork to one of fat, season it very high with pepper and salt, add a small quantity of dried sage rubbed to a powder, have the skins nicely prepared, fill them and hang them in a dry place. Sausages are excellent made into cakes and fried, but will not keep so well as in skins.

## TO MAKE BLACK PUDDINGS.

CATCH the blood as it runs from the hog, stir it continually till cold to prevent its coagulating; when cold thicken it with boiled rice or oatmeal, add leaf fat chopped small, pepper, salt, and any herbs that are liked, fill the skins and smoke them two or three days; they must be boiled before they are hung up, and prick them with a fork to keep them from bursting.

## A SEA PIE.

LAY at the bottom of a small Dutch oven some slices of boiled pork or salt beef, then potatos and onions cut in slices, salt, pepper, thyme and parsley shred fine, some crackers soaked, and a layer of fowls cut up, or slices of veal; cover them with a paste not too rich, put another layer of each article, and cover them with paste until the oven is full; put a little butter between each layer, pour in water till it reaches the top crust, to which you must add wine, catsup of any kind you please, and some pounded cloves; let it stew until there is just gravy enough left; serve it in a deep dish and pour the gravy on.

## TO MAKE PASTE FOR THE PIE.

POUR half a pound of butter or dripping, boiling hot, into a quart of flour, add as much water as will make it a paste, work it and roll it well before you use it. It is quite a savoury paste.

## BOLOGNA SAUSAGES.

TAKE one pound of bacon—fat and lean, one ditto veal, do., pork, do., suet, chop all fine, season highly: fill the skins, prick and boil them an hour, and hang them to dry—grated bread or boiled rice may be added: clean the skins with salt and vinegar.

# FISH.

### TO CURE HERRINGS.

THE best method for preserving herrings, and which may be followed with ease, for a small family, is to take the brine left of your winter stock for beef, to the fishing place, and when the seine is hauled, to pick out the largest herrings, and throw them alive into the brine; let them remain twenty-four hours, take them out and lay them on sloping planks, that the brine may drain off; have a tight barrel, put some coarse alum salt at the bottom, then put in a layer of herrings—take care not to bruise them; sprinkle over it alum salt and some saltpetre, then fish, salt, and saltpetre, till the barrel is full; keep a board over it. Should they not make brine enough to cover them in a few weeks, you must add some, for they will be rusty if not kept under brine. The proper time to salt them is when they are quite fat: the scales will adhere closely to a lean herring, but will be loose on a fat one—the former is not fit to be eaten. Do not be sparing of salt when you put them up. When they are to be used, take a few out of brine, soak them an hour or two, scale them nicely, pull off the gills, and the only entrail they have will come with them; wash them clean and hang them up to dry. When to be broiled, take half a sheet of white paper, rub it over with butter, put the herring in, double the edges securely, and broil without burning it. The brine the herrings drink before they die, has a wonderful effect in preserving their juices: when one or two years old, they are equal to anchovies.

## TO BAKE STURGEON.

GET a piece of sturgeon with the skin on, the piece next to the tail, scrape it well, cut out the gristle, and boil it about twenty minutes to take out the oil; take it up, pull off the large scales, and when cold, stuff it with forcemeat, made of bread crumbs, butter, chopped parsley, pepper and salt, put it in a Dutch oven just large enough to hold it, with a pint and a half of water, a gill of red wine, one of mushroom catsup, some salt and pepper, stew it gently till the gravy is reduced to the quantity necessary to pour over it; take up your sturgeon carefully, thicken the gravy with a spoonful of butter rubbed into a large one of brown flour;—see that it is perfectly smooth when you put it in the dish.

## TO MAKE STURGEON CUTLETS.

THE tail piece is the best; skin it and cut off the gristle, cut it into slices about half an inch thick, sprinkle over them pepper and salt, dredge them with flour, and fry them a nice light brown; have ready a pint of good gravy, seasoned with catsup, wine, and a little pounded cloves, and thickened with brown flour and butter; when the cutlets are cold, put them into the gravy and stew them a few minutes; garnish the dish with nice forcemeat balls and parsley fried crisp.

## STURGEON STEAKS.

CUT them as for the cutlets, dredge them, and fry them nicely; dish them quickly lest they get cold;

pour ovei melted butter with chopped parsley, and garnish with fried parsley.

## TO BOIL STURGEON.

LEAVE the skin on, which must be nicely scraped, take out the gristle, rub it with salt, and let it lie an hour, then put it on in cold water with some salt and a few cloves of garlic; it must be dredged with flour before it is put into the water, skim it carefully, and when dished, pour over it melted butter with chopped parsley, a large spoonful of mushroom catsup, one of lemon pickle, and one of pepper vinegar; send some of it to table in a sauce boat;—the sturgeon being a dry fish, rich sauce is necessary.

## TO BAKE A SHAD.

THE shad is a very indifferent fish unless it be large and fat; when you get a good one, prepare it nicely, put some forcemeat inside, and lay it at full length in a pan with a pint of water, a gill of red wine, one of mushroom catsup, a little pepper, vinegar, salt, a few cloves of garlic, and six cloves: stew it gently till the gravy is sufficiently reduced; there should always be a fish-slice with holes to lay the fish on, for the convenience of dishing without breaking it; when the fish is taken up, slip it carefully into the dish; thicken the gravy with butter and brown flour, and pour over it.

## TO BOIL A SHAD.

GET a nice fat shad, fresh from the water, that the skin may not crack in boiling, put it in cold water on a slice, in a kettle of proper length, with a wine

glass of pale vinegar, salt, a little garlic, and a bundle of parsley; when it is done, drain all the water
from the fish, lay it in the dish, and garnish with
scraped horse-radish; have a sauce boat of nice melted
butter, to mix with the different catsups, as taste shall
direct.

## TO ROAST A SHAD.

FILL the cavity with good forcemeat, sew it up, and
tie it on a board of proper size, cover it with bread
crumbs, with some salt and pepper, set it before the
fire to roast; when done on one side, turn it, tie it
again, and when sufficiently done, pull out the thread,
and serve it up with butter and parsley poured over it.

## TO BROIL A SHAD.

SEPARATE one side from the back-bone, so that it
will lie open without being split in two; wash it clean,
dry it with a cloth, sprinkle some salt and pepper on
it, and let it stand till you are ready to broil it; have
the gridiron hot and well greased, broil it nicely, and
pour over it melted butter.

## TO BOIL ROCK FISH.

THE best part of the rock is the head and shoulders—clean it nicely, put it into the fish kettle with
cold water and salt, boil it gently and skim it well;
when done, drain off the water, lay it in the dish, and
garnish with scraped horse-radish; have two boats of
butter nicely melted with chopped parsley, or for a
change, you may have anchovy butter; the roe and
liver should be fried and served in separate dishes. If
any of the rock be left, it will make a delicious dish

next day;—pick it in small pieces, put it in a stew
pan with a gill of water, a good lump of butter, some
salt, a large spoonful of lemon pickle, and one of
pepper vinegar—shake it over the fire till perfectly
hot, and serve it up. It is almost equal to stewed
crab.

## TO FRY PERCH.

CLEAN the fish nicely, but do not take out the roes;
dry them on a cloth, sprinkle some salt, and dredge
them with flour, lay them separately on a board; when
one side is dry, turn them, sprinkle salt and dredge
the other side; be sure the lard boils when you put
the fish in, and fry them with great care; they should
be a yellowish brown when done. Send melted butter or anchovy sauce in a boat.

## TO PICKLE OYSTERS.

SELECT the largest oysters, drain off their liquor,
and wash them in clean water; pick out the pieces of
shells that may be left, put them in a stew pan with
water proportioned to the number of oysters, some
salt, blades of mace, and whole black pepper; stew
them a few minutes, then put them in a pot, and when
cold, add as much pale vinegar as will give the
liquor an agreeable acid.

## TO MAKE A CURRY OF CATFISH.

TAKE the white channel catfish, cut off their heads,
skin and clean them, cut them in pieces four inches
long, put as many as will be sufficient for a dish into
a stew pan with a quart of water, two onions, and
chopped parsley; let them stew gently till the water

is reduced to half a pint, take the fish out and lay
them on a dish, cover them to keep them hot, rub a
spoonful of butter into one of flour, add a large tea-
spoonful of curry powder, thicken the gravy with it,
shake it over the fire a few minutes, and pour it over
the fish; be careful to have the gravy smooth.

## TO DRESS A COD'S HEAD AND SHOULDERS.

TAKE out the gills and the blood from the bone,
wash the head very clean, rub over it a little salt, then
lay it on your fish plate; throw in the water a good
handful of salt, with a glass of vinegar, then put in
the fish, and let it boil gently half an hour; if it is a
large one, three quarters; take it up very carefully,
strip the skin nicely off, set it before a brisk fire,
dredge it all over with flour, and baste it well with
butter; when the froth begins to rise, throw over it
some very fine white bread crumbs; you must keep
basting it all the time to make it froth well; when it
is a fine light brown, dish it up, and garnish it with a
lemon cut in slices, scraped horse-radish, barberries,
a few small fish fried and laid around it, or fried
oysters—cut the roe and liver in slices, and lay over
it a little of the lobster out of the sauce in lumps, and
then serve it up.

## TO MAKE SAUCE FOR THE COD'S HEAD.

TAKE a lobster, if it be alive, stick a skewer in the
vent of the tail, (to keep the water out,) throw a
handful of salt in the water; when it boils, put in the
lobster, and boil it half an hour; if it has spawn on it,

pick them off, and pound them exceedingly fine in a marble mortar, and put them into half a pound of good melted butter, then take the meat out of the lobster, pull it in bits, and put it in your butter, with a meat spoonful of lemon pickle, and the same of walnut catsup, a slice of lemon, one or two slices of horse-radish, a little beaten mace, salt and cayenne to your taste; boil them one minute, then take out the horse-radish and lemon, and serve it up in your sauce boat.

N. B. If you cannot get lobsters, you may make shrimp, cockle, or muscle sauce, the same way; if there can be no shell fish got, you then may add two anchovies cut small, a spoonful of walnut liquor, a large onion stuck with cloves—strain and put it in the sauce boat.

----

## TO DRESS A SALT COD.

Steep your salt fish in water all night, with a glass of vinegar; it will take out the salt, and make it taste like fresh fish; the next day boil it; when it is enough take off the skin, pull it in fleaks into your dish, then pour egg sauce over it, or parsnips boiled and beat fine, with butter and cream; send it to the table on a water plate, for it will soon grow cold.

----

## MATELOTE OF ANY KIND OF FIRM FISH.

Cut the fish in pieces six inches long, put it in a pot with onion, parsley, thyme, mushrooms, a little spice, pepper and salt—add red wine and water enough for gravy, set it on a quick fire and reduce it one-third, thicken with a spoonful of butter and two of flour; put it in a dish with bits of bread fried in butter, and pour the gravy over it.

## CHOWDER, A SEA DISH.

TAKE any kind of firm fish, cut it in pieces six inches long, sprinkle salt and pepper over each piece, cover the bottom of a small Dutch oven with slices of salt pork about half boiled, lay in the fish, strewing a little chopped onion between; cover with crackers that have been soaked soft in milk, pour over it two gills of white wine, and two of water; put on the top of the oven, and stew it gently about an hour; take it out carefully, and lay it in a deep dish; thicken the gravy with a little flour and a spoonful of butter, add some chopped parsley, boil it a few minutes, and pour it over the fish—serve it up hot.

## TO PICKLE STURGEON.

THE best sturgeons are the small ones, about four feet long without the head, and the best part is the one near the tail. After the sturgeon is split through the back bone, take a piece with the skin on, which is essential to its appearance and goodness, cut off the gristle, scrape the skin well, wash it, and salt it—let it lie twenty-four hours, wipe off the salt, roll it, and tie it around with twine, put it on in a good deal of cold water, let it boil till you can run a straw easily into the skin, take it up, pull off the large scales, and when cold, put it in a pot, and cover it with one part vinegar, and two of salt and water; keep it closely stopped, and when served, garnish with green fennel.

## TO CAVEACH FISH.

CUT the fish in pieces the thickness of your hand, wash it and dry it in a cloth, sprinkle on some pepper and salt, dredge it with flour, and fry it a nice brown; when it gets cold, put it in a pot with a little chopped onion between the layers, take as much vinegar and water as will cover it, mix with it some oil, pounded mace, and whole black pepper, pour it on, and stop the pot closely. This is a very convenient article, as it makes an excellent and ready addition to a dinner or supper. When served up, it should be garnished with green fennel, or parsley.

## TO DRESS COD FISH.

BOIL the fish tender, pick it from the bones, take an equal quantity of Irish potatos, or parsnips boiled and chopped, and the same of onions well boiled; add a sufficiency of melted butter, some grated nutmeg, pepper, and salt, with a little brandy or wine; rub them in a mortar till well mixed; if too stiff, liquify it with cream or thickened milk, put paste in the bottom of a dish, pour in the fish, and bake it. For change, it may be baked in the form of patties.

## COD FISH PIE.

SOAK the fish, boil it and take off the skin, pick the meat from the bones, and mince it very fine; take double the quantity of your fish, of stale bread grated; pour over it as much new milk, boiling hot, as will wet it completely, add minced parsley, nutmeg, pepper, and made mustard, with as much melted butter as will make it sufficiently rich; the quantity must be determined by that of the other ingredients—beat these together very well, add the minced fish, mix it all, cover the bottom of the dish with good paste, pour the fish in, put on a lid and bake it.

## TO DRESS ANY KIND OF SALTED FISH.

TAKE the quantity necessary for the dish, wash them, and lay them in fresh water for a night; then put them on the tin plate with holes, and place it in the fish kettle—sprinkle over it pounded cloves and pepper, with four cloves of garlic; put in a bundle of sweet herbs and parsley, a large spoonful of tarragon, and two of common vinegar, with a pint of wine; roll one quarter of a pound of butter in two spoonsful of flour, cut it in small pieces, and put it over the fish—cover it closely, and simmer it over a slow fire half an hour; take the fish out carefully, and lay it in the dish, set it over hot water, and cover it till the gravy has boiled a little longer—take out the garlic and herbs, pour it over the fish, and serve it up. It is very good when eaten cold with salad, garnished with parsley.

## TO FRICASSEE COD SOUNDS AND TONGUES.

SOAK them all night in fresh water, take off the skins, cut them in two pieces, and boil them in milk and water till quite tender, drain them in a colander, and season with nutmeg, pepper, and a little salt—take as much new milk as will make sauce for it, roll a good lump of butter in flour, melt it in the milk, put the fish in, set it over the fire, and stir it till thick enough, and serve it up.

## AN EXCELLENT WAY TO DRESS FISH.

DREDGE the fish well with flour, sprinkle salt and pepper on them, and fry them a nice brown; set them by to get cold; put a quarter of a pound of butter in a frying pan; when it boils, fry tomatos with the skins taken off, parsley nicely picked, and a very little chopped onion; when done, add as much water as will make sauce for the fish—season it with pepper, salt, and pounded cloves; add some wine and mushroom catsup, put the fish in, and when thoroughly heated, serve it up.

## FISH A-LA-DAUB.

BOIL as many large white perch as will be sufficient. for the dish; do not take off their heads, and be careful not to break their skins; when cold, place them in the dish, and cover them with savoury jelly broken. A nice piece of rock-fish is excellent done in the same way.

## FISH IN JELLY.

FILL a deep glass dish half full of jelly—have as many small fish-moulds as will lie conveniently in it fill them with blanc mange; when they are cold, and the jelly set, lay them on it, as if going in different directions; put in a little more jelly, and let it get cold, to keep the fish in their places—then fill the dish so as to cover them. The jelly should be made of hog's feet, very light coloured, and perfectly transparent.

## TO MAKE EGG SAUCE FOR A SALT COD.

BOIL four eggs hard, first half cnop the white, then put in the yelks, and chop them both together, but not very small; put them into half a pound of good melted butter, and let it boil up—then pour it on the fish.

## TO DRESS COD SOUNDS.

STEEP your sounds as you do the salt cod, and boil them in a large quantity of milk and water; when they are very tender and white, take them up, and drain the water out and skin them; then pour the egg sauce boiling hot over them, and serve them up.

## TO STEW CARP.

GUT and scale your fish, wash and dry them well with a clean cloth, dredge them with flour, fry them in lard until they are a light brown, and then put them in a stew pan with half a pint of water, and half a pint of red wine, a meat spoonful of lemon pickle, the same of walnut catsup, a little mushroom powder and cayenne to your taste, a large onion stuck with cloves, and a stick of horse-radish; cover your pan close up to keep in the steam; let them stew gently over a stove fire, till the gravy is reduced to just enough to cover your fish in the dish; then take the fish out, and put them on the dish you intend for the table, set the gravy on the fire, and thicken it with flour, and a large lump of butter; boil it a little, and strain it over your fish; garnish them wi'n pickled mushrooms and scraped horse-radish, and send them to the table.

___

## TO BOIL EELS.

CLEAN the eels, and cut off their heads, dry them, and turn them round on your fish plate, boil them in salt and water, and make parsley sauce for them.

___

## TO PITCHCOCK EELS.

SKIN and wash your eels, then dry them with a cloth, sprinkle them with pepper, salt, and a little dried sage, turn them backward and forward, and skewer them; rub a gridiron with beef suet, broil them a nice brown, put them on a dish with good melted butter, and lay around fried parsley.

___

## TO BROIL EELS.

WHEN you have skinned and cleansed your eels as before, rub them with the yelk of an egg, strew over them bread crumbs, chopped parsley, sage, pepper, and salt; baste them well with butter, and set them in a dripping pan; serve them up with parsley and butter for sauce.

___

## TO SCOLLOP OYSTERS.

WHEN the oysters are opened, put them in a bowl, and wash them out of their own liquor; put some in the scollop shells, strew over them a few bread crumbs, and lay a slice of butter on them, then more oysters, bread crumbs, and a slice of butter on the top; put them into a Dutch oven to brown, and serve them up in the shells.

## TO FRY OYSTERS.

TAKE a quarter of a hundred of large oysters, wash them and roll them in grated bread, with pepper and salt, and fry them a light brown; if you choose, you may add a little parsley, shred fine. They are a proper garnish for calves' head, or most made dishes.

## TO MAKE OYSTER LOAVES.

TAKE little round loaves, cut off the tops, scrape out all the crumbs, then put the oysters into a stew pan with the crumbs that came out of the loaves, a little water, and a good lump of butter; stew them together ten or fifteen minutes, then put in a spoonful of good cream, fill your loaves, lay the bit of crust carefully on again, set them in the oven to crisp. Three are enough for a side dish.

# POULTRY, &c.

## TO ROAST A GOOSE.

CHOP a few sage leaves and two onions very fine. mix them with a good lump of butter, a tea-spoonful of pepper, and two of salt, put it in the goose, then spit it, lay it down, and dust it with flour; when it is thoroughly hot, baste it with nice lard; if it be a large one, it will require an hour and a half, before a good clear fire; when it is enough, dredge and baste it, pull out the spit, and pour in a little boiling water.

## TO MAKE SAUCE FOR A GOOSE.

PARE, core and slice some apples; put them in a sauce pan, with as much water as will keep them from burning, set them over a very slow fire, keep them closely covered till reduced to a pulp, then put in a lump of butter, and sugar to your taste, beat them well, and send them to the table in a china bowl.

## TO BOIL DUCKS WITH ONION SAUCE.

SCALD and draw your ducks, put them in warm water for a few minutes, then take them out and put them in an earthen pot; pour over them a pint of boiling milk, and let them lie in it two or three hours; when you take them out, dredge them well with flour, and put them in a copper of cold water; put on the cover, let them boil slowly twenty minutes, then take them out, and smother them with onion sauce.

## TO MAKE ONION SAUCE.

BOIL eight or ten large onions, change the water two or three times while they are boiling; when enough, chop them on a board to keep them a good colour, put them in a sauce pan with a quarter of a pound of butter and two spoonsful of thick cream; boil it a little, and pour it over the ducks.

## TO ROAST DUCKS.

WHEN you have drawn the ducks, shred one onion and a few sage leaves, put them into the ducks with pepper and salt, spit and dust them with flour, and baste them with lard: if your fire be very hot, they will roast in twenty minutes; and the quicker they are roasted, the better they will taste. Just before you take them from the spit, dust them with flour and baste them  Get ready some gravy made of the gizzards and pinions, a large blade of mace, a few pepper corns, a spoonful of catsup, a tea-spoonful of lemon pickle; strain it and pour it on the ducks, and send onion sauce in a boat.

## TO BOIL A TURKEY WITH OYSTER SAUCE.

GRATE a loaf of bread, chop a score or more of oysters fine, add nutmeg, pepper and salt to your taste, mix it up into a light forcemeat with a quarter of a pound of butter, a spoonful or two of cream, and three eggs; stuff the craw with it, and make the rest into balls and boil them; sew up the turkey, dredge it well with flour, put it in a kettle of cold water, cover it, and set it over the fire; as the scum begins to rise, take it off, let it boil very slowly for half an hour, then take off your kettle and keep it closely covered; if it be of a middle size, let it stand in the hot water half an hour, the steam being kept in, will stew it enough, make it rise, keep the skin whole, tender, and very white; when you dish it, pour on a little oyster sauce, lay the balls round, and serve it up with the rest of the sauce in a boat.

N. B. Set on the turkey in time, that it may stew as above; it is the best way to boil one to perfection. Put it over the fire to heat, just before you dish it up.

## TO MAKE SAUCE FOR A TURKEY.

As you open the oysters, put a pint into a bowl, wash them out of their own liquor, and put them in another bowl; when the liquor has settled, pour it off into a sauce pan with a little white gravy, and a tea-spoonful of lemon pickle—thicken it with flour and a good lump of butter; boil it three or four minutes, put in a spoonful of good cream, add the oysters, keep shaking them over the fire till they are quite hot, but don't let them boil, for it will make them hard and appear small.

---

## TO ROAST A TURKEY.

MAKE the forcemeat thus: take the crumb of a loaf of bread, a quarter of a pound of beef suet shred fine, a little sausage meat or veal scraped and pounded very fine, nutmeg, pepper, and salt to your taste; mix it lightly with three eggs, stuff the craw with it, spit it, and lay it down a good distance from the fire, which should be clear and brisk; dust and baste it several times with cold lard; it makes the froth stronger than basting it with the hot out of the drip-ping pan, and makes the turkey rise better; when it is enough, froth it up as before, dish it, and pour on the same gravy as for the boiled turkey, or bread sauce; garnish with lemon and pickles, and serve it up; if it be of a middle size, it will require one hour and a quarter to roast.

---

## TO MAKE SAUCE FOR A TURKEY.

CUT the crumb of a loaf of bread in thin slices, and put it in cold water with a few pepper corns, a little salt and onion—then boil it till the bread is quite soft, beat it well, put in a quarter of a pound of butter, two spoonsful of thick cream, and put it in the dish with the turkey.

---

## TO BOIL FOWLS.

DUST the fowls well with flour, put them in a kettle of cold water, cover it close, set it on the fire; when the scum begins to rise, take it off, let them boil very slowly for twenty minutes, then take them off, cover them close, and the heat ot the water wili stew them enough in half an hour; it keeps the skin whole, and they will be both whiter and plumper than if they had boiled fast; when you take them up, drain them, and pour over them white sauce or melted butter.

---

## TO MAKE WHITE SAUCE FOR FOWLS.

TAKE a scrag of veal, the necks of fowls, or any bits of mutton or veal you have; put them in a sauce pan with a blade or two of mace, a few black pepper corns, one anchovy, a head of celery, a bunch of sweet herbs, a slice of the end of a lemon; put in a quart of water, cover it close, let it boil till it is reduced to half a pint, strain it, and thicken it with a quarter of a pound of butter mixed with flour, boil it five or six minutes, put in two spoonsful of pickled mushrooms, mix the yelks of two eggs with a tea cup full of good cream and a little nutmeg—put it in the sauce, keep shaking it over the fire, but don't let it boil.

## FRICASSEE OF SMALL CHICKENS.

TAKE off the legs and wings of four chickens, separate the breasts from the backs, cut off the necks and divide the backs across, clean the gizzards nicely, put them with the livers and other parts of the chicken, after being washed clean, into a sauce pan, add pepper, salt, and a little mace, cover them with water, and stew them till tender—then take them out, thicken half a pint of the water with two table spoonsful of flour rubbed into four ounces of butter, add half a pint of new milk, boil all together a few minutes, then add a gill of white wine, stirring it in carefully that it may not curdle; put the chickens in, and continue to shake the pan until they are sufficiently hot, and serve them up.

## TO ROAST LARGE FOWLS.

TAKE the fowls when they are ready dressed, put them down to a good fire, dredge and baste them well with lard; they will be near an hour in roasting; make a gravy of the necks and gizzards, strain it, put in a spoonful of brown flour; when you dish them, pour on the gravy, and serve them up with egg sauce in a boat.

## TO MAKE EGG SAUCE.

BOIL four eggs for ten minutes, chop half the whites, put them with the yelks, and chop them both together, but not very fine; put them into a quarter of a pound of good melted butter, and put it in a boat.

## TO BOIL YOUNG CHICKENS.

PUT the chickens in scalding water; as soon as the feathers will slip off, take them out, or it will make the skin hard and break: when you have drawn them, lay them in skimmed milk for two. hours, then truss and dust them well with flour, put them in cold water, cover them close, set them over a very slow fire, take off the scum, let them boil slowly for five or six minutes, take them off the fire, keep them closely covered in the water for half an hour, it will stew them enough; when you are going to dish them, set them over the fire to make them hot, drain them, and pour over white sauce made the same way as for the boiled fowls.

## TO ROAST YOUNG CHICKENS.

WHEN you kill young chickens, pluck them very carefully, truss and put them down to a good fire, dredge and baste them with lard; they will take a quarter of an hour in roasting; froth them up, lay them on the dish, pour butter and parsley on, and serve them up hot.

## FRIED CHICKENS.

CUT them up as for the fricassee, dredge them well with flour, sprinkle them with salt, put them into a good quantity of boiling lard, and fry them a light brown; fry small pieces of mush and a quantity of parsley nicely picked, to be served in the dish with the chickens; take half a pint of rich milk, add to it a small bit of butter, with pepper, salt, and chopped parsley; stew it a little, and pour it over the chickens, and then garnish with the fried parsley.

---

### TO ROAST WOODCOCKS OR SNIPES.

PLUCK, but do not draw them, put them on a small spit, dredge and baste them well with lard, toast a few slices of bread, put them on a clean plate, and set it under the birds while they are roasting; if the fire be good, they will take about ten minutes; when you take them from the spit, lay them upon the toasts on the dish, pour melted butter round them, and serve them up.

---

### TO ROAST WILD DUCKS OR TEAL.

WHEN the ducks are ready dressed, put in them a small onion, pepper, salt, and a spoonful of red wine; if the fire be good, they will roast in twenty minutes; make gravy of the necks and gizzards, a spoonful of red wine, half an anchovy, a blade or two of mace, one onion, and a little cayenne pepper; boil it till it is wasted to half a pint, strain it through a hair sieve, and pour it on the ducks—serve them up with onion sauce in a boat; garnish the dish with raspings of bread.

---

### TO BOIL PIGEONS.

SCALD the pigeons, draw them, take the craw out, wash them in several waters, cut off the pinions, turn the legs under the wings, dredge them, and put them in soft cold water; boil them slowly a quarter of an hour, dish them up, pour over them good melted butter, lay round a little brocoli in bunches, and send butter and parsley in a boat.

## TO ROAST PIGEONS.

WHEN you have dressed your pigeons as before, roll a good lump of butter in chopped parsley, with pepper and salt, put it in your pigeons, spit, dust and baste them; if the fire be good, they will roast in twenty minutes; when they are enough, lay round them bunches of asparagus, with parsley and butter for sauce.

## TO ROAST PARTRIDGES OR ANY SMALL BIRDS.

LARD them with slips of bacon, put them on a skewer, tie it to the spit at both ends, dredge and baste them, let them roast ten minutes, take the grated crumb of half a loaf of bread, with a piece of butter, the size of a walnut, put it in a stew pan, and shake it over a gentle fire till it is of a light brown, lay it between your birds, and pour over them a little melted butter.

## TO BROIL RABBITS.

WHEN you have cased the rabbits, skewer them with their heads straight up, the fore-legs brought down, and the hind-legs straight; boil them three quarters of an hour at least, then smother them with onion sauce, made the same as for boiled ducks, and serve them up.

## TO ROAST RABBITS.

WHEN you have cased the rabbits, skewer their heads with their mouths upon their backs, stick their fore-legs into their ribs, skewer the hind-legs doubled, then make a pudding for them of the crumb of half a loaf of bread, a little parsley, sweet marjoram and thyme, all shred fine, nutmeg, salt and pepper to your taste, mix them up into a light stuffing, with a quarter of a pound of butter, a little good cream, and two eggs; put it into the body, and sew them up; dredge and baste them well with lard, roast them near an hour, serve them up with parsley and butter for sauce, chop the livers, and lay them in lumps round the edge of the dish.

## TO STEW WILD DUCKS.

HAVING prepared the fowls, rub the insides with salt, pepper, and a little powdered cloves; put a shallot or two with a lump of butter in the body of each, then lay them in a pan that will just hold them, putting butter under and over them, with vinegar and water, and add pepper, salt, lemon peel, and a bunch of sweet herbs; then cover the pan close, and let them stew till done—pass the liquor through a sieve, pour it over the ducks, and serve them up hot, with a garnish of lemon sliced, and raspings of bread fried. The same way may teal, &c. be dressed.

## TO DRESS DUCKS WITH JUICE OF ORANGES.

The ducks being singed, picked, and drawn, mince the livers with a little scraped bacon, some butter, green onions, sweet herbs and parsley, seasoned with salt, pepper, and mushrooms; these being all minced together, put them into the bodies of the ducks, and roast them, covered with slices of bacon, and wrapped up in paper; then put a little gravy, the juice of an orange, a few shallots minced, into a stew pan, and shake in a little pepper; when the ducks are roasted, take off the bacon, dish them, and pour your sauce with the juice of oranges over them, and serve them up hot.

## TO DRESS DUCKS WITH ONIONS.

Stuff the ducks as before, cut the roots off small onions, blanch them in scalding water, then pick and put them into a stew pan with a little gravy, set them over a gentle fire, and let them simmer; when they are done, thicken them with cream and flour, and when the ducks are roasted, dish them, pour the ragout of onions over, and serve them up hot.

## TO ROAST A CALF'S HEAD.

Wash and pick the head very nicely; having taken out the brains and tongue, prepare a good quantity of forced meat, with veal and suet well seasoned; fill the hole of the head with this forced meat, skewer and tie it together upon the spit, and roast it for an hour and a half. Beat up the brains with a little sage and parsley shred fine, a little salt, and the yelks of two or three eggs; boil the tongue, peel, and cut it into large dice, fry that with the brains, also some of the forced meat made up into balls, and slices of bacon. Let the sauce be strong gravy, with oysters, mushrooms, capers, and a little white wine thickened.

## TO MAKE A DISH OF CURRY AFTER THE EAST INDIAN MANNER.

Cut two chickens as for fricassee, wash them clean, and put them in a stew pan with as much water as will cover them; sprinkle them with a large spoonful of salt, and let them boil till tender, covered close all the time, and skim them well; when boiled enough, take up the chickens, and put the liquor of them into a pan, then put half a pound of fresh butter in the pan, and brown it a little; put into it two cloves of garlic, and a large onion sliced, and let these all fry till brown, often shaking the pan; then put in the chickens, and sprinkle over them two or three spoonsful of curry powder; then cover the pan close, and let the chickens do till brown, often shaking the pan; then put in the liquor the chickens were boiled in, and let all stew till tender; if acid is agreeable squeeze the juice of a lemon or orange in it.

## DISH OF RICE TO BE SERVED UP WITH THE CURRY, IN A DISH BY ITSELF.

Take half a pound of rice, wash it clean in salt and water—then put it into two quarts of boiling water, and boil it briskly twenty minutes; strain it through a colander and shake it into a dish, but do not touch it with your fingers nor with a spoon.

Beef, veal, mutton, rabbits, fish, &c. may be curried and sent to table with or without the dish of rice.

Curry powder is used as a fine flavoured seasoning for fish, fowls, steaks, chops, veal cutlets, hashes, minces, alamodes, turtle soup, and in all rich dishes, gravies, sauce, &c. &c.

## OCHRA AND TOMATOS.

TAKE an equal quantity of each, let the ochra be young, slice it, and skin the tomatos; put them into a pan without water, add a lump of butter, an onion chopped fine, some pepper and salt, and stew them one hour.

## GUMBO—A WEST INDIA DISH.

GATHER young pods of ochra, wash them clean, and put them in a pan with a little water, salt and pepper, stew them till tender, and serve them with melted butter. They are very nutritious, and easy of digestion.

## PEPPER POT.

BOIL two or three pounds of tripe, cut it in pieces, and put it on the fire with a knuckle of veal, and a sufficient quantity of water; part of a pod of pepper, a little spice, sweet herbs according to your taste, salt, and some dumplins; stew it till tender, and thicken the gravy with butter and flour.

## SPANISH METHOD OF DRESSING GIBLETS.

TAKE the entrails of fat full grown fowls, empty them of their contents—open them with a sharp knife, scrape off the inner coat; wash them clean, and put them on to boil with the liver, gizzard, and other giblets; add salt, pepper, and chopped onion—when quite tender, set them by to cool; put some nice dripping or butter in a pan, when it boils put the giblets, add salt, fry them a nice brown; when nearly done, break six eggs in a bowl, beat them a little, pour them over the giblets, stir them for a few minutes, and serve them up.

## PASTE FOR MEAT DUMPLINS.

CHOP half a pound of suet very fine—add one and a quarter pound of flour, and a little salt—mix it up with half a pint of milk, knead it till it looks light; take a bowl of proper size, rub the inside with butter, roll out the paste and lay it in; parboil beef steaks, mutton-chops, or any kind of meat you like; season it and lay it in the bowl—fill it with rich gravy, close the paste over the top—get a very thick cloth that will keep out the water; wet and flour it, place it over the top of the bowl—gather it at bottom and tie it very securely; the water must boil when you put it in—when done, dip the top in cold water for a moment, that the cloth may not stick to the paste; untie and take it off carefully—put a dish on the bowl and turn it over—if properly made, it will come out without breaking; have gravy in a boat to eat with it.

## TO MAKE AN OLLO—A SPANISH DISH.

TAKE two pounds beef, one pound mutton, a chicken, or half a pullet, and a small piece of pork; put them into a pot with very little water, and set it on the fire at ten o'clock, to stew gently; you must sprinkle over it an onion chopped small, some pepper and salt, before you pour in the water; at half after twelve, put into the pot two or three apples or pears, peeled and cut in two, tomatos with the skin taken off, cimblins cut in pieces, a handful of mint chopped, lima beans, snaps, and any kind of vegetable you like; let them all stew together till three o'clock; some cellery tops cut small, and added at half after two, will improve it much.

## ROPA VEIJA—SPANISH.

PEEL the skin from ripe tomatos, put them in a pan with a spoonful of melted butter, some pepper and salt, shred cold meat or fowl; put it in, and fry it sufficiently.

## CHICKEN PUDDING, A FAVOURITE VIRGINIA DISH.

BEAT ten eggs very light, add to them a quart of rich milk, with a quarter of a pound of butter melted, and some pepper and salt; stir in as much flour as will make a thin good batter; take four young chickens, and after cleaning them nicely, cut off the legs, wings, &c. put them all in a sauce pan, with some salt and water, and a bundle of thyme and parsley, boil them till nearly done, then take the chicken from the water and put it in the batter pour it in a deep dish, and bake it; send nice white gravy in a boat

---

### TO MAKE POLENTA.

Put a large spoonful of butter in a quart of water, wet your corn meal with cold water in a bowl, add some salt, and make it quite smooth, then put it in the buttered water when it is hot, let it boil, stirring it continually till done; as soon as you can handle it, make it into a ball, and let it stand till quite cold— then cut it in thin slices, lay them in the bottom of a deep dish so as to cover it, put on it slices of cheese, and on that a few bits of butter; then mush, cheese and butter, until the dish is full; put on the top thin slices of cheese and butter, put the dish in a quick oven; twenty or thirty minutes will bake it.

---

### MACARONI.

Boil as much macaroni as will fill your dish, in milk and water, till quite tender; drain it on a sieve sprinkle a little salt over it, put a layer in your dish then cheese and butter as in the polenta, and bake it in the same manner.

---

### MOCK MACARONI.

Break some crackers in small pieces, soak them in milk until they are soft; then use them as a substitute for macaroni.

## TO MAKE CROQUETS.

TAKE cold fowl or fresh meat of any kind, with slices of ham, fat and lean—chop them together very fine, add half as much stale bread grated, salt, pepper, grated nutmeg, a teaspoonful of made mustard, a table-spoonful of catsup, and a lump of butter; knead all well together till it resembles sausage meat, make them in cakes, dip them in the yelk of an egg beaten, cover them thickly with grated bread, and fry them a light brown.

## TO MAKE VERMECELLI.

BEAT two or three fresh eggs quite light, make them into a stiff paste with flour, knead it well, and roll it out very thin, cut it in narrow strips, give them a twist, and dry them quickly on tin sheets. It is an excellent ingredient in most soups, particularly those that are thin. Noodles are made in the same manner, only instead of strips they should be cut in tiny squares and dried. They are also good in soups

## COMMON PATTIES.

TAKE some veal, fat and lean, and some slices of boiled ham, chop them very fine, and season it with salt, pepper, grated nutmeg, and a small quantity of parsley and thyme minced very fine; with a little gravy make some paste, cover the bottoms of small moulds, fill them with the meat, put thin lids on, and bake them crisp; five is enough for a side dish

## EGGS IN CROQUETS.

Boil eighteen eggs, separate the yelks and whites, and cut them in dice; pour over them a sauce a-la-creme, (*see sauce a-la-creme*,) add a little grated bread, mix all well together, and let it get cold; put in some salt and pepper, make them into cakes, cover them well on both sides with grated bread, let them stand an hour, and fry them a nice brown; dry them a little before the fire, and dish them while quite hot.

## OMELETTE SOUFFLE.

Break six eggs, beat the yelks and whites separately till very light, then mix them, add four table spoonsful of powdered sugar, and a little grated lemon peel; put a quarter of a pound of butter in a pan; when melted, pour in the eggs and stir them; when they have absorbed the butter, turn it on a plate previously buttered, sprinkle some powdered sugar, set it in a hot Dutch oven, and when a little brown, serve it up for a desert.

## FONDUS.

Put a pint of water, and a lump of butter the size of an egg, into a sauce pan; stir in as much flour as will make a thick batter, put it on the fire, and stir it continually till it will not stick to the pan; put it in a bowl, add three quarters of a pound of grated cheese, mix it well, then break in two eggs, beat them well, then two more until you put in six; when it ooks very light, drop it in small lumps on buttered paper, bake it in a quick oven till of a delicate brown; you may use corn meal instead of flour for a change.

---

## A NICE TWELVE O'CLOCK LUNCHEON.

CUT some slices of bread tolerably thick, and toast them slightly; bone some anchovies, lay half of one on each toast, cover it well with grated cheese and chopped parsley mixed; pour a little melted butter on, and brown it with a salamander; it must be done on the dish you send it to table in.

---

## EGGS A-LA-CREME.

BOIL twelve eggs just hard enough to allow you to cut them in slices—cut some crusts of bread very thin, put them in the bottom and round the sides of a moderately deep dish, place the eggs in, strewing each layer with the stale bread grated, and some pepper and salt.

---

## SAUCE A-LA-CREME, FOR THE EGGS.

PUT a quarter of a pound of butter, with a large tablespoonful of flour rubbed well into it in a sauce pan; add some chopped parsley, a little onion, salt, pepper, nutmeg, and a gill of cream; stir it over the fire until it begins to boil, then pour it over the eggs, cover the top with grated bread, set it in a Dutch oven with a heated top, and when a light brown, send it to table

## CABBAGE A-LA-CREME.

TAKE two good heads of cabbage, cut out the stalks, boil it tender, with a little salt in the water—have ready one large spoonful of butter, and a small one of flour rubbed into it, half a pint of milk, with pepper and salt; make it hot, put the cabbage in after pressing out the water, and stew it till quite tender.

## TO MAKE AN OMELETTE.

BREAK six or eight eggs in a dish, beat them a little, add parsley and chives chopped small, with pepper and salt; mix all well together, put a piece of butter in a pan, let it melt over a clear fire till nearly brown; pour in the eggs, stir it in, and in a few minutes it will be done sufficiently; double it, and dish it quite hot.

## OMELETTE—ANOTHER WAY.

BREAK six eggs, leave out half the whites—beat them with a fork, and add some salt and chopped parsley; take four ounces of fresh butter, cut half of it in small pieces, put them in the omelette, put the other half in a small frying pan; when melted, pour in the eggs; stir till it begins to set, then turn it up round the edges; when done, put a plate on and turn the pan up, that it may not break—the omelette must be thick, and great care must be taken in frying; instead of parsley, you may use any kind of sweet herb or onion chopped fine, anchovy minced, rasped beef, ham or tongue.

## GASPACHO—SPANISH

PUT some soft biscuit or toasted bread in the bottom of a sallad bowl, put in a layer of sliced tomatos with the skin taken off, and one of sliced cucumbers, sprinkled with pepper, salt, and chopped onion; do this until the bowl is full; stew some tomatos quite soft, strain the juice, mix in some mustard, oil, and water, and pour over it; make it two hours before it is eaten.

## EGGS AND TOMATOS.

PEEL the skins from a dozen large tomatos, put four ounces of butter in a frying pan, add some salt, pepper, and a little chopped onion; fry them a few minutes, add the tomatos, and chop them while frying; when nearly done, break in six eggs, stir them quickly, and serve them up.

## TO FRICASSEE EGGS.

BOIL six eggs for five minutes, lay them in cold water, peel them carefully, dredge them lightly with flour, beat one egg light, dip the hard eggs in, roll them in bread crumbs, seasoned with pepper, salt, and grated nutmeg; cover them well with this, and let them stand some time to dry—fry them in boiling lard, and serve them up with any kind of rich, well seasoned gravy, and garnish with crisped parsley.

# SAUCES.

### FISH SAUCE, TO KEEP A YEAR.

CHOP twenty-four anchovies, bones and all, two shallots, a handful of scraped horse radish, four blades of mace, one quart of white wine, one pint of anchovy liquor, one pint of claret, twelve cloves, and twelve pepper corns; boil them together till reduced to a quart, then strain it off into a bottle for use Two spoonsful will be sufficient for a pound of butter

### SAUCE FOR WILD FOWL.

TAKE a gill of claret, with as much water, some grated bread, three heads of shallots, a little whole pepper, mace, grated nutmeg, and salt; let them stew over the fire, then beat it up with butter, and put it under the wild fowl, which being a little roasted, will afford gravy to mix with this sauce.

### SAUCE FOR BOILED RABBITS.

BOIL the livers, and shred them very small, chop two eggs not boiled very hard, a large spoonful of grated white bread, some broth, sweet herbs, two spoonsful of white wine, one of vinegar, a little salt, and some butter; stir all together, and take care the butter does not oil.

### GRAVY,

TAKE a rasher or two of bacon, and lay it at the bottom of a stew pan, putting either veal, mutton, or beef, cut in slices, over it; then add some sliced onions, turnips, carrots, celery, a little thyme, and alspice. Put in a little water, and set it on the fire, stewing till it be brown at the bottom, which you will know from the pan's hissing; then pour boiling water over it, and stew it an hour and a half; but the time must be regulated by the quantity. Season it with salt and pepper.

## FORCEMEAT BALLS.

TAKE half a pound of veal, and half a pound of suet cut fine, and beat in a marble mortar or wooden bowl; add a few sweet herbs shred fine, a little mace pounded fine, a small nutmeg grated, a little lemon peel, some pepper and salt, and the yelks of two eggs; mix them well together, and make them into balls and long pieces—then roll them in flour, and fry them brown. If they are for the use of white sauce, do not fry them, but put them in a sauce-pan of hot water and let them boil a few minutes.

## SAUCE FOR BOILED DUCKS OR RABBITS

POUR boiled onions over your ducks, or rabbits, prepared in this manner: peel some onions, and boil them in plenty of water; then change the first water, and boil them two hours: take them up and put them in a colander to drain, and afterwards chop them on a board: then put them in a sauce-pan, sprinkle a little flour over them, and put in a large piece of butter, with a little milk or cream. Set them over the fire,

and when the butter is melted, they will be done
enough. This is a good sauce for mutton also.

## LOBSTER SAUCE.

Boil a little mace, and whole pepper, long enough
to take out the strong taste of the spice; then strain
it off, and melt three quarters of a pound of butter in
it. Cut the lobster in very small pieces, and stew it
till it is tender.

## SHRIMP SAUCE.

Wash half a pint of shrimps very clean—mince
and put them in a stew-pan, with a spoonful of anchovy liquor, and a pound of thick melted butter;
boil it up for five minutes, and squeeze in half a
lemon. Toss it up, and put it in a sauce-boat.

## OYSTER SAUCE FOR FISH.

Scald a pint of oysters, and strain them through a
sieve; then wash some more in cold water, and take
off their beards; put them in a stew-pan, and pour
the liquor over them; then add a large spoonful of
anchovy liquor, half a lemon, two blades of mace,
and thicken it with butter rolled in flour. Put in half
a pound of butter, and boil it till it is melted—take
out the mace and lemon, and squeeze the lemon juice
into the sauce; boil it, and stir it all the time, and
put it in a boat.

## CELERY SAUCE.

Wash and pare a large bunch of celery very clean
cut it into little bits, and boil it softly till it is tender;

add half a pint of cream, some mace, nutmeg, and a small piece of butter rolled in flour; then boil it gently. This is a good sauce for roasted or boiled fowls, turkeys, partridges, or any other game.

## MUSHROOM SAUCE.

CLEAN and wash one quart of fresh mushrooms, cut them in two, and put them into a stew-pan, with a little salt, a blade of mace, and a little butter; stew them gently for half an hour, and then add half a pint of cream, and the yelks of two eggs beat very well— keep stirring it till it boils up. Put it over the fowls or turkies—or you may put it on a dish with a piece of fried bread first buttered—then toasted brown, and just dipped into boiling water. This is very good sauce for white fowls of all kinds.

## COMMON SAUCE.

PLAIN butter melted thick, with a spoonful of walnut pickle or catsup, is a very good sauce; but you may put as many things as you choose into sauces.

## TO MELT BUTTER.

NOTHING is more simple than this process, and nothing so generally done badly. Keep a quart tin sauce-pan, with a cover to it, exclusively for this purpose; weigh one quarter of a pound of good butter; rub into it two tea-spoonsful of flour; when well mixed, put it in the sauce-pan with one table-spoonful of water, and a little salt; cover it, and set the sauce-pan in a larger one of boiling water; shake it constantly till completely melted, and beginning to boil. If the pan containing the butter be set on coals, it will oil the butter and spoil it. This quantity is sufficient for one sauce-boat. A great variety of delicious sauces can be made, by adding different herbs to melted butter, all of which are excellent to eat with fish, poultry, or boiled butchers' meat. To begin with parsley—wash a large bunch very clean, pick the leaves from the stems carefully, boil them ten minutes in salt and water, drain them perfectly dry, mince them exceedingly fine, and stir them in the butter when it begins to melt. When herbs are added to butter, you must put two spoonsful of water instead of one. Chervil, young fennel, burnet, tarragon, and cress, or peppergrass, may all be used, and must be prepared in the same manner as the parsley.

---

### CAPER SAUCE,

Is made by mixing a sufficient quantity of capers. and adding them to the melted butter, with a little of the liquor from the capers; where capers cannot be obtained, pickled nasturtiums make a very good substitute, or even green pickle minced and put with the butter.

---

### OYSTER CATSUP.

GET fine fresh oysters, wash them in their own liquor, put them in a marble mortar with salt, pounded mace, and cayenne pepper, in the proportions of one ounce salt, two drachms mace, and one of cayenne to each pint of oysters; pound them together, and add a pint of white wine to each pint; boil it some minutes, and rub it through a sieve; boil it again, skim it, and when cold, bottle, cork, and seal it. This composition gives a fine flavour to white sauces, and if a glass of brandy be added, it will keep good for a considerable time.

## CELERY VINEGAR.

Pound two gills of celery seed, put it into a bottle and fill it with strong vinegar; shake it every day for a fortnight, then strain it, and keep it for use. It will impart a pleasant flavour of celery to any thing with which it is used. A very delicious flavour of thyme may be obtained, by gathering it when in full perfection; it must be picked from the stalks, a large hand ful of it put into a jar, and a quart of vinegar or brandy poured on it; cover it very close—next day, take all the thyme out, put in as much more; do this a third time; then strain it, bottle and seal it securely. This is greatly preferable to the dried thyme commonly used, during the season when it cannot be obtained in a fresh state. Mint may be prepared in the same way. The flavour of both these herbs must be preserved by care in the preparation: if permitted to stand more than twenty hours in the liquor they are infused in, a coarse and bitter taste will be extracted, particularly from mint.

# VEGETABLES.

## TO DRESS SALAD.

To have this delicate dish in perfection, the lettuce, pepper grass, chervil, cress, &c. should be gathered early in the morning, nicely picked, washed, and laid in cold water, which will be improved by adding ice; just before dinner is ready to be served, drain the water from your salad, cut it into a bowl, giving the proper proportions of each plant; prepare the following mixture to pour over it: boil two fresh eggs ten minutes, put them in water to cool, then take the yelks in a soup plate, pour on them a table spoonful of cold water, rub them with a wooden spoon until they are perfectly dissolved; then add two spoonsful of oil: when well mixed, put in a teaspoonful of salt, one of powdered sugar, and one of made mustard; when all these are united and quite smooth, stir in two table spoonsful of common, and two of tarragon vinegar; put it over the salad, and garnish the top with the whites of the eggs cut into rings, and lay around the edge of the bowl young scallions, they being the most delicate of the onion tribe.

## TO BOIL POTATOS.

Wash them, but do not pare or cut them, unless they are very large; fill a sauce-pan half full of potatos of equal size, (or make them so by dividing the large ones,) put to them as much cold water as will cover them about an inch; they are sooner boiled, and more savoury, than when drowned in water; most boiled things are spoiled by having too little water, but potatos are often spoiled by having too much; they must merely be covered, and a little allowed for waste in boiling, so that they must be just covered when done. Set them on a moderate fire till they boil, then take them off, and set them by the fire to simmer slowly, till they are soft enough to admit a fork; (place no dependence on the usual test of their skin's cracking, which, if they are boiled fast, will happen to some potatos when they are not half done, and the inside is quite hard,) then pour off the water, (if you let the potatos remain in the water a moment after they are done enough, they will become waxy and watery,) uncover the sauce-pan, and set it at such a distance from the fire as will secure it from burning; their superfluous moisture will evaporate, and the potatos will be perfectly dry and mealy. You may afterwards place a napkin, folded up to the size of the sauce-pan's diameter, over the potatos, to keep them dry and mealy till wanted, this method of managing potatos, is, in every respect, equal to steaming them, and they are dressed in half the time.

## TO FRY SLICED POTATOS.

PEEL large potatos, slice them about a quarter of an inch thick, or cut them in shavings round and round, as you would peel a lemon; dry them well in a clean cloth, and fry them in lard or dripping. Take care that your fat and frying-pan are quite clean; put it on a quick fire, watch it, and as soon as the lard boils and is still, put in the slices of potatos, and keep moving them till they are crisp; take them up, and lay them to drain on a sieve; send them up with very little salt sprinkled on them.

## POTATOS MASHED.

WHEN the potatos are thoroughly boiled, drain and dry them perfectly, pick out every speck, and rub them through a colander into a clean stew-pan; to a pound of potatos put half an ounce of butter, and a tablespoonful of milk; do not make them too moist; mix them well together. When the potatos are getting old and specked, and in frosty weather, this is the best way of dressing them—you may put them into shapes, touch them over with yelk of egg, and brown them very slightly before a slow fire.

## POTATOS MASHED WITH ONIONS.

PREPARE some onions by putting them through a sieve, and mix them with potatos; in proportioning the onions to the potatos, you will be guided by your wish to have more or less of their flavour.

## TO ROAST POTATOS.

WASH and dry your potatos, (all of a size,) and put them in a tin Dutch oven, or cheese toaster; take care not to put them too near the fire, or they will get burned on the outside before they are warmed through. Large potatos will require two hours to roast them. To save time and trouble, some cooks half boil them first.

## TO ROAST POTATOS UNDER MEAT.

HALF boil large potatos, drain the water from them, and put them into an earthen dish or small tin pan,

under meat that is roasting, and baste them with some
of the dripping; when they are browned on one side,
turn them and brown the other; send them up around
the meat, or in a small dish.

## POTATO BALLS.

Mix mashed potatos with the yelk of an egg, roll
them into balls, flour them, or cover them with egg
and bread crumbs, fry them in clean dripping, or
brown them in a Dutch oven. They are an agreeable
vegetable relish, and a supper dish.

## JERUSALEM ARTICHOKES,

Are boiled and dressed in the various ways we have
just before directed for potatos. They should be
covered with thick melted butter, or a nice white or
brown sauce.

## CABBAGE.

Pick cabbages very clean, and wash them thoroughly; then look them carefully over again; quarter
them if they are very large; put them into a sauce pan
with plenty of boiling water; if any skum rises, take
it off, put a large spoonful of salt into the sauce pan,
and boil them till the stalks feel tender. A young
cabbage will take about twenty minutes, or half an
hour; when full grown, nearly an hour; see that they
are well covered with water all the time, and that no
dirt or smoke arises from stirring the fire. With

careful management, they will look as beautiful when
dressed as they did when growing. It will much
ameliorate the flavour of strong old cabbages, to boil
them in two waters, *i. e.* when they are half done, to
take them out, and put them into another sauce pan
of boiling water.

## SAVOYS,

ARE boiled in the same manner; quarter them when
you send them to table.

## SPROUTS AND YOUNG GREENS

THE receipt written for cabbages will answer as
well for sprouts, only they will be boiled enough in
fifteen minutes.

## ASPARAGUS.

SET a stew-pan with plenty of water on the fire,
sprinkle a handful of salt in it, let it boil, and skim it;
then put in the asparagus prepared thus: scrape all the
stalks till they are perfectly clean; throw them into a
pan of cold water as you scrape them; when they are
all done, tie them in little bundles, of a quarter of a
hundred each, with bass, if you can get it, or tape; cut
off the stalks at the bottom, that they may be all of a
length; when they are tender at the stalk, which
will be in from twenty to thirty minutes, they are
done enough. Great care must be taken to watch the
exact time of their becoming tender; take them just
at that instant, and they will have their true flavour
and colour; a minute or two more boiling destroys

both. While the asparagus is boiling, toast a slice of a loaf of bread, about a half an inch thick; brown it delicately on both sides; dip it lightly in the liquor the asparagus was boiled in, and lay it in the middle of a dish; pour some melted butter on the toast, and lay the asparagus upon it; let it project beyond the asparagus, that the company may see there is a toast. Do not pour butter over them, but send some in a boat.

## SEA-KALE,

Is tied up in bundles, and dressed in the same way as asparagus.

## TO SCOLLOP TOMATOS.

PEEL off the skin from large, full, ripe tomatos—put a layer in the bottom of a deep dish, cover it well with bread grated fine; sprinkle on pepper and salt, and lay some bits of butter over them—put another layer of each, till the dish is full—let the top be covered with crumbs and butter—bake it a nice brown.

## TO STEW TOMATOS.

TAKE off the skin, and put them in a pan with salt, pepper, and a large piece of butter—stew them till sufficiently dry.

## CAULIFLOWER.

CHOOSE those that are close and white, and of a middle size—trim off the outside leaves, cut off the

stalk flat at the bottom, let them lie in salt and water
an hour before you boil them. Put them in boiling
water, with a handful of salt in it—skim it well, and
let it boil slowly till done, which a small one will be
in fifteen minutes, a large one in twenty—and take it
up the moment it is enough: a few minutes longer
boiling will spoil it.

## RED BEET ROOTS,

ARE not so much used as they deserve to be; they
are dressed in the same way as parsnips, only neither
scraped nor cut till after they are boiled; they will
take from an hour and a half to three hours in boiling,
according to their size; to be sent to the table with
salt fish, boiled beef, &c. When young, small and
juicy, it is a very good variety, an excellent garnish,
and easily converted into a very cheap and pleasant
pickle.

## PARSNIPS,

ARE to be cooked just in the same manner as carrots; they require more or less time, according to their
size; therefore match them in size, and you must try
them by thrusting a fork into them as they are in the
water; when this goes easily through, they are done
enough: boil them from an hour to two hours, according to their size and freshness. Parsnips are
sometimes sent up mashed in the same way as
turnips.

## CARROTS.

LET them be well washed and scraped—an hour is enough for young spring carrots; grown carrots will take from an hour and a half to two hours and a half. The best way to try if they are done enough, is to pierce them with a fork.

## TURNIPS.

PEEL off half an inch of the stringy outside—full grown turnips will take about an hour and a half gentle boiling; try them with a fork, and when tender, take them up, and lay them on a sieve till the water is thoroughly drained from them; send them up whole; to very young turnips, leave about two inches of green top; the old ones are better when the water is changed as directed for cabbage.

## TO MASH TURNIPS.

WHEN they are boiled quite tender, squeeze them as dry as possible—put them into a sauce pan, mash them with a wooden spoon, and rub them through a colander; add a little bit of butter, keep stirring them till the butter is melted and well mixed with them, and they are ready for table.

## TURNIP TOPS,

ARE the shoots which grow out, (in the spring,) from the old turnip roots. Put them in cold water an hour before they are dressed; the more water they are boiled in, the better they will look; if boiled in a small quantity of water, they will taste bitter; when the water boils, put in a small handful of salt, and then your vegetables; they are still better boiled with bacon in the Virginia style: if fresh and young, they will be done in about twenty minutes—drain them on the back of a sieve, and put them under the bacon.

### FRENCH BEANS.

Cut off the stalk end first, and then turn to the point and strip off the strings; if not quite fresh, have a bowl of spring water, with a little salt dissolved in it, standing before you; as the beans are cleansed and trimmed, throw them in; when all are done, put them on the fire in boiling water, with some salt in it; when they have boiled fifteen or twenty minutes, take one out and taste it; as soon as they are tender, take them up, and throw them into a colander to drain. To send up the beans whole, when they are young, is much the best method, and their delicate flavour and colour is much better preserved. When a little more grown, they must be cut lengthwise in thin slices after stringing; and for common tables, they are split, and divided across; but those who are nice, do not use them at such a growth as to require splitting.

### ARTICHOKES.

Soak them in cold water, wash them well, then put them into plenty of boiling water, with a handful of salt, and let them boil gently till they are tender, which will take an hour and a half, or two hours: the surest way to know when they are done enough, is to draw out a leaf; trim them, and drain them on a sieve, and send up melted butter with them, with some put into small cups, so that each guest may have one.

## BROCOLI.

THE kind which bears flowers around the joints of the stalks, must be cut into convenient lengths for the dish; scrape the skin from the stalk, and pick out any leaves or flowers that require to be removed; tie it up in bunches, and boil it as asparagus; serve it up hot, with melted butter poured over it. The brocoli that heads at the top like cauliflowers, must be dressed in the same manner as the cauliflower.

## PEAS.

To have them in perfection, they must be quite young, gathered early in the morning, kept in a cool place, and not shelled until they are to be dressed; put salt in the water, and when it boils, put in the peas; boil them quick twenty or thirty minutes, according to their age; just before they are taken up, add a little mint chopped very fine; drain all the water from the peas, put in a bit of butter, and serve them up quite hot.

## PUREE OF TURNIPS.

PARE a dozen large turnips, slice them, and put them into a stew-pan, with four ounces of butter and a little salt; set the pan over a moderate fire, turn

them often with a wooden spoon; when they look
white, add a ladle full of veal gravy, stew them till
it becomes thick; skim it, and pass it through a sieve;
put the turnips in a dish, and pour the gravy over
them.

### RAGOUT OF TURNIPS.

Peel as many small turnips as will fill a dish; put
them into a stew pan with some butter and a little
sugar, set them over a hot stove, shake them about,
and turn them till they are a good brown; pour
in half a pint of rich high seasoned gravy; stew the
turnips till tender, and serve them with the gravy
poured over them.

### RAGOUT OF FRENCH BEANS, SNAPS, STRING BEANS.

Let them be young and fresh gathered, string them,
and cut them in long thin slices; throw them in boiling water for fifteen minutes; have ready some well
seasoned brown gravy, drain the water from the beans,
put them in the gravy, stew them a few minutes, and
serve them garnished with forcemeat balls; there must
not be gravy enough to float the beans.

### MAZAGAN BEANS.

This is the smallest and most delicate species of
the Windsor bean. Gather them in the morning,
when they are full grown, but quite young, and do
not shell them till you are going to dress them. Put
them into boiling water, have a small bit of middling,

(flitch,) of bacon, well boiled—take the skin off, cover it with bread crumbs, and toast it; lay this in the middle of the dish, drain all the water from the beans—put a little butter with them, and pour them round the bacon. When the large Windsor beans are used, it is best to put them into boiling water until the skins will slip off, and then make them into a puree as directed for turnips—they are very coarse when plainly dressed.

## LIMA, OR SUGAR BEANS.

LIKE all other spring and summer vegetables, they must be young and freshly gathered: boil them till tender, drain them, add a little butter, and serve them up. These beans are easily preserved for winter use, and will be nearly as good as fresh ones. Gather them on a dry day, when full grown, but quite young: have a clean and dry keg, sprinkle some salt in the bottom, put in a layer of pods, containing the beans, then a little salt—do this till the keg is full; lay a board on with a weight, to press them down; cover the keg very close, and keep it in a dry, cool place—they should be put up as late in the season, as they can be with convenience. When used, the pods must be washed, and laid in fresh water all night; shell them next day, and keep them in water till you are going to boil them; when tender, serve them up with melted butter in a boat. French beans (snaps) may be preserved in the same manner.

## TURNIP ROOTED CABBAGE.

THE cabbage growing at the top is not good; cut the root in slices an inch thick, peel off the rind, and boil the slices in a large quantity of water, till tender, serve it up hot, with melted butter poured over it.

## EGG PLANT.

THE purple ones are best; get them young and fresh; pull out the stem, and parboil them to take off the bitter taste; cut them in slices an inch thick, but do not peel them; dip them in the yelk of an egg, and cover them with grated bread, a little salt and pepper—when this has dried, cover the other side the same way—fry them a nice brown. They are very delicious, tasting much like soft crabs. The egg plant may be dressed in another manner: scrape the rind and parboil them; cut a slit from one end to the other, take out the seeds, fill the space with a rich forcemeat, and stew them in well seasoned gravy, or bake them, and serve up with gravy in the dish.

## POTATO PUMPKIN

GET one of a good colour, and seven or eight inches in diameter; cut a piece off the top, take out all the seeds, wash and wipe the cavity, pare the rind off, and fill the hollow with good forcemeat—put the top on, and set it in a deep pan, to protect the sides; bake it in a moderate oven, put it carefully in the dish without breaking, and it will look like a handsome mould. Another way of cooking potato pumpkin is to cut it in slices, pare off the rind, and make a puree as directed for turnips.

## SWEET POTATO.

TAKE those that are nearly of the same size, that they may be done equally—wash them clean, but do not peel them—boil them till tender, drain the water off, and put them on tin sheets in a stove for a few minutes to dry.

---

## SWEET POTATOS STEWED.

WASH and wipe them, and if they be large, cut them in two lengths; put them at the bottom of a stew pan, lay over some slices of boiled ham; and on that, one or two chickens cut up with pepper, salt, and a bundle of herbs; pour in some water, and stew them till done, then take out the herbs, serve the stew in a deep dish—thicken the gravy, and pour over it.

---

## SWEET POTATOS BROILED.

CUT them across without peeling, in slices half an inch thick, broil them on a griddle, and serve them with butter in a boat.

---

## SPINACH.

GREAT care must be used in washing and picking it clean; drain it, and throw it into boiling water—a few minutes will boil it sufficiently: press out all the water, put it in a stew pan with a piece of butter, some pepper and salt—chop it continually with a spoon till it is quite dry: serve it with poached eggs or without, as you please.

---

## SORREL.

Is dressed as the spinach; and if they be mixed in equal proportions, improve each other.

## CABBAGE PUDDING.

GET a fine head of cabbage, not too large; pour boiling water on, and cover it till you can turn the leaves back, which you must do carefully; take some of those in the middle of the head off, chop them fine, and mix them with rich forcemeat; put this in, and replace the leaves to confine the stuffing—tie it in a cloth, and boil it—serve it up whole, with a little melted butter in the dish.

## SQUASH OR CIMLIN.

GATHER young squashes, peel, and cut them in two; take out the seeds, and boil them till tender; put them into a colander, drain off the water, and rub them with a wooden spoon through the colander; then put them into a stew pan, with a cup full of cream, a small piece of butter, some pepper and salt—stew them, stirring very frequently until dry. This is the most delicate way of preparing squashes.

## WINTER SQUASH.

THE crooked neck of this squash is the best part. Cut it in slices an inch thick, take off the rind, and boil them with salt in the water; drain them well before they are dished, and pour melted butter over—serve them up very hot.

The large part, containing the seeds, must be sliced and pared—cut it in small pieces, and stew it till soft, with just water enough to cover it; pass it through a sieve and stew it again, adding some butter, pepper, and salt; it must be dry, but not burnt. It is excellent when stewed with pork chops.

## FIELD PEAS.

THERE are many varieties of these peas; the smaller kind are the most delicate. Have them young and newly gathered, shell and boil them tender; pour them in a colander to drain; put some lard in a frying pan; when it boils, mash the peas, and fry them in a cake of a light brown; put it in the dish with the crust uppermost—garnish with thin bits of fried bacon. They are very nice when fried whole, so that each pea is distinct from the other; but they must be boiled less, and fried with great care. Plain boiling is a very common way of dressing them.

## CABBAGE WITH ONIONS.

BOIL them separately, and mix them in the proportions you like; add butter, pepper, and salt, and either stew them, or fry them in a cake.

## SALSIFY.

SCRAPE and wash the roots, put them into boiling water with salt; when done, drain them, and place them in the dish without cutting them up. They are a very excellent vegetable, but require nicety in cooking; exposure to the air, either in scraping, or after boiling, will make them black.

## STEWED SALSIFY.

HALF boil it, cut it up, and put it in a stew pan, with a very little water, and a spoonful of butter; stew them dry, and serve them up. For change, you may, after stewing, cut them in scollop shells with grated bread, and bake them; or make them into cakes, and fry them. They are delicious in whatever way they can be dressed.

---

### STEWED MUSHROOMS.

GATHER grown mushrooms, but such as are young enough to have red gills; cut off that part of the stem which grew in the earth—wash them carefully, and take the skin from the top; put them into a stew pan with some salt, but no water—stew them till tender, and thicken them with a spoonful of butter, mixed with one of brown flour; red wine may be added, but the flavour of the mushroom is too delicious to require aid from any thing.

---

### BROILED MUSHROOMS.

PREPARE them as above directed—broil them on a griddle, and when done, sprinkle pepper and salt on the gills, and put a little butter on them.

---

### TO BOIL RICE.

PUT two cups full of rice in a bowl of water, rub it well with the hand, and pour off the water; do this until the water ceases to be discoloured; then put the rice into two and a half cups of cold water; add a tea-spoonful of salt, cover the pot close, and set it on a brisk fire; let it boil ten minutes, pour off the greater part of the water, and remove the pot to a bed of coals, where it must remain a quarter of an hour to soak and dry.

### RICE JOURNEY, OR JOHNNY CAKE.

Boil a pint of rice quite soft, with a tea-spoonful of salt; mix with it while hot a large spoonful of butter, and spread it on a dish to cool; when perfectly cold, add a pint of rice flour and half a pint of milk—beat them all together till well mingled. Take the middle part of the head of a barrel, make it quite clean, wet it, and put on the mixture about an inch thick, smooth with a spoon, and baste it with a little milk; set the board aslant before clear coals; when sufficiently baked, slip a thread under the cake and turn it: baste and bake that side in a similar manner, split it, and butter while hot. Small homony boiled and mixed with rice flour, is better than all rice; and if baked very thin, and afterwards toasted and buttered, it is nearly as good as cassada bread.

# PUDDINGS, &c.

### OBSERVATIONS ON PUDDINGS AND CAKES

The salt should always be washed from butter, when it is to be used in any thing that has sugar for an ingredient, and also from that which is melted to grease any kind of mould for baking—otherwise, there will be a disagreeable salt taste on the outer side of the article baked. Raisins should be stoned and cut in two, and have some flour sifted over them—stir them gently in the flour, and take them out free from lumps; the small quantity that adheres to them, will prevent their sticking together, or falling in a mass to the bottom. Eggs must be fresh, or they will not beat well: it is better to separate the yelks from the whites always, though it is a more troublesome process; but for some things it is essential to do so: when they are to be mixed with milk, let it cool after boiling, or the eggs will poach; and only set it on the fire a few minutes, to take off the raw taste of the eggs, stirring it all the time. Currants require washing in many waters to cleanse them; they must be picked and well dried, or they will stick together. Almonds should be put in hot water till the skins will slip off, which is called blanching; they must always be pounded with rose or orange flower water, to prevent their oiling. When cream is used, put it in just before the mixture is ready; much beating will decompose it. Before a pudding or cake is begun, every ingredient necessary for it must be ready; when the process is retarded by neglecting to have them prepared, the article is injured. The oven must be in a proper state, and the paste in the dishes or moulds, ready for such things as require it. Promptitude is necessary in all our actions, but never more so than when engaged in making cakes and puddings. When only one or two eggs are to be used, cooks generally think it needless to beat them—it is an error: eggs injure every thing, unless they are made light before they are used. Cloths for boiling puddings should be made of German sheeting; an article less thick, will admit the water, and injure the pudding.

## RICE MILK FOR A DESSERT.

Boil half a pint of rice in water till tender pour off the water, and add a pint of milk with two eggs beaten well, stirred into it; boil all together two or three minutes; serve it up hot, and eat it with butter, sugar, and nutmeg. It may be sweetened and cooled in moulds, turned out in a deep dish, and surrounded with rich milk, with raspberry marmalade stirred into it, and strained to keep back the seeds—or the milk may be seasoned with wine and sugar.

## TO MAKE PUFF PASTE.

Sift a quart of flour, leave out a little for rolling the paste, make up the remainder with cold water into a stiff paste, knead it well, and roll it out several times; wash the salt from a pound of butter, divide it into four parts, put one of them on the paste in little bits, fold it up, and continue to roll it till the butter is well mixed; then put another portion of butter, roll it in the same manner; do this till all the butter is mingled with the paste; touch it very lightly with the hands in making—bake it in a moderate oven, that will permit it to rise, but will not make it brown. Good paste must look white, and as light as a feather.

## TO MAKE MINCEMEAT FOR PIES.

Boil either calves or hogs' feet till perfectly tender, rub them through a colander; when cold, pass them through again, and it will come out like pearl barley;

take one quart of this, one of chopped apples, the same of currants, washed and picked, raisins stoned and cut, of good brown sugar, suet nicely chopped, and cider, with a pint of brandy; add a tea-spoonful of pounded mace, one of cloves and of nutmegs; mix all these together intimately. When the pies are to be made, take out as much of this mixture as may be necessary; to each quart of it, add a tea-spoonful of pounded black pepper, and one of salt; this greatly improves the flavour, and can be better mixed with a small portion than with the whole mass. Cover the moulds with paste, put in a sufficiency of mincemeat, cover the top with citron sliced thin, and lay on it a lid garnished around with paste cut in fanciful shapes. They may be eaten either hot or cold, but are best when hot.

----

## TO MAKE JELLY FROM FEET.

Boil four calfs' feet, that have been nicely cleaned, and the hoofs taken off; when the feet are boiled to pieces, strain the liquor through a colander, and when cold, take all the grease off, and put the jelly in a skillet, leaving the dregs which will be at the bottom. There should be from four feet, about two quarts of jelly: pour into it one quart of white wine, the juice of six fresh lemons strained from the seeds, one pound and a half of powdered loaf sugar, a little pounded cinnamon and mace, and the rind thinly pared from two of the lemons; wash eight eggs very clean, whip up the whites to a froth, crush the shells and put with them, mix it with the jelly, set it on the fire, stir it occasionally till the jelly is melted, but do not touch

it afterwards. When it has boiled till it looks quite clear on one side, and the dross accumulates on the other, take off carefully the thickest part of the dross, and pour the jelly in the bag; put back what runs through, until it becomes quite transparent—then set a pitcher under the bag, and put a cover all over to keep out the dust: the jelly looks much prettier when it is broken to fill the glasses. The bag should be made of cotton or linen, and be suspended in a frame made for the purpose. The feet of hogs make the palest coloured jelly; those of sheep are a beautiful amber-colour, when prepared.

## A SWEETMEAT PUDDING.

MAKE a quart of flour into puff paste; when done, divide it into three parts of unequal size; roll the largest out square and moderately thin, spread over it a thin layer of marmalade, leaving a margin all round about an inch broad; roll the next largest in the same manner, lay it on, cover that with marmalade, leaving a margin; then roll the smallest, and put it on the other two, spreading marmalade; fold it up, one fold over the other, the width of your hand—press the ends together, tie it in a cloth securely, and place it in a kettle of boiling water, where it can lie at length without doubling; boil it quickly, and when done, pour melted butter with sugar and wine in the dish.

## TO MAKE AN ORANGE PUDDING.

PUT two oranges and two lemons, into five quarts of water—boil them till the rinds are quite tender;

take them out, and when cold, slice them thin, and
pick out the seeds; put a pound of loaf sugar into a
pint of water—when it boils, slice into it twelve
pippins pared and cored—lay in the lemons and
oranges, stew them tender, cover the dish with puff
paste, lay the fruit in carefully, in alternate layers—
pour on the syrup, put some slips of paste across,
and bake it.

## AN APPLE CUSTARD.

PARE and core twelve pippins, slice them tolerably
thick, put a pound of loaf sugar in a stew pan, with
a pint of water and twelve cloves: boil and skim it,
then put in the apples, and stew them till clear, and
but little of the syrup remains—lay them in a deep
dish, and take out the cloves; when the apples are
cold, pour in a quart of rich boiled custard—set it in
water, and make it boil till the custard is set—take
care the water does not get into it.

## BOILED LOAF.

POUR a quart of boiling milk over four little rolls of
bread—cover them up, turning them occasionally till
saturated with the milk; tie them very tight in cloths,
and boil them an hour; lay them in the dish, and pour
a little melted butter over them; for sauce, have but
ter in a boat, seasoned with wine, sugar, and grated
nutmeg.

## TRANSPARENT PUDDING.

BEAT eight eggs very light, add half a pound of
pounded sugar, the same of fresh butter melted, and

half a nutmeg grated; sit it on a stove, and keep stirring till it is as thick as buttered eggs—put a puff paste in a shallow dish, pour in the ingredients, and bake it half an hour in a moderate oven; sift sugar over it, and serve it up hot.

## FLUMMERY.

ONE measure of jelly, one of cream, and half a one of wine; boil it fifteen minutes over a slow fire, stirring all the time; sweeten it, and add a spoonful of orange flower or rose water; cool it in a mould, turn it in a dish, and pour around it cream, seasoned in any way you like.

## BURNT CUSTARD.

BOIL a quart of milk—and when cold, mix with it the yelks of eight eggs; stir them together over the fire a few minutes; sweeten it to your taste, put some slices of savoy cake in the bottom of a deep dish, and pour on the custard; whip the whites of the eggs to a strong froth, lay it lightly on the top, sift some sugar over it, and hold a salamander over it until it is a light brown; garnish the top with raspberry marmalade, or any kind of preserved fruit.

## AN ENGLISH PLUM PUDDING.

BEAT eight eggs very light, add to them a pound of flour sifted, and a pound of powdered sugar; when it looks quite light, put in a pound of suet finely shred, a pint of milk, a nutmeg grated, and a gill of brandy;

mix with it a pound of currants, washed, picked, and dried, and a pound of raisins stoned and floured—tie it in a thick cloth, and boil it steadily eight hours.

## MARROW PUDDING.

Grate a large loaf of bread, and pour on the crumbs a pint of rich milk boiling hot; when cold, add four eggs, a pound of beef marrow sliced thin, a gill of brandy, with sugar and nutmeg to your taste—mix all well together, and either bake or boil it· when done, stick slices of citron over the top.

## SIPPET PUDDING.

Cut a loaf of bread as thin as possible, put a layer of it in the bottom of a deep dish, strew on some slices of marrow or butter, with a handful of currants or stoned raisins; do this till the dish is full; let the currants or raisins be at the top; beat four eggs, mix with them a quart of milk that has been boiled a little and become cold, a quarter of a pound of sugar, and a grated nutmeg—pour it in, and bake it in a moderate oven—eat it with wine sauce.

## SWEET POTATO PUDDING.

Boil one pound of sweet potatos very tender, rub them while hot through a colander; add six eggs well beaten, three quarters of a pound of powdered sugar, three quarters of butter, and some grated nutmeg and lemon peel, with a glass of brandy; put a paste in the dish, and when the pudding is done, sprinkle the top with sugar, and cover it with bits of citron. Irish potato pudding is made in the same manner, but is not so good.

## AN ARROW ROOT PUDDING.

Boil a quart of milk, and make it into a thick batter, with arrow root; add six eggs, half a pound of butter, the same of pounded sugar, half a nutmeg, and a little grated lemon peel; put a paste in the dish, and bake it nicely; when done, sift sugar over it, and stick slips of citron all over the top.

## SAGO PUDDING.

Wash half a pound of sago in several waters; put it on to boil in a quart of milk, with a stick of cinnamon; stir it very frequently, for it is apt to burn: when it becomes quite thick, take out the cinnamon, stir it in half a pound of butter, and an equal quantity of sugar, with a gill of wine; when cold, add six eggs and four ounces of currants that have been plumped in hot water—bake it in a paste.

## PUFF PUDDING.

Beat six eggs, add six spoonsful of milk, and six of flour, butter some cups, pour in the batter, and bake them quickly; turn them out, and eat them with butter, sugar and nutmeg.

## RICE PUDDING.

Boil half a pound of rice in milk, until it is quite tender; beat it well with a wooden spoon to mash the grains; add three quarters of a pound of sugar, and the same of melted butter; half a nutmeg, six eggs, a gill of wine, and some grated lemon peel; put a paste in the dish, and bake it. For change, it may be boiled, and eaten with butter, sugar, and wine.

## PLUM PUDDING.

Take a pound of the best flour, sift it, and make it up before sunrise, with six eggs beaten light; a large spoonful of good yeast, and as much milk as will make it the consistence of bread; let it rise well, knead into it half a pound of butter, put in a grated nutmeg, with one and a half pounds of raisins stoned and cut up; mix all well together, wet the cloth, flour it, and tie it loosely, that the pudding may have room to rise. Raisins for puddings or cakes, should be rubbed in a little flour, to prevent their settling to the bottom—see that it does not stick to them in lumps.

## ALMOND PUDDING.

Put a pound of sweet almonds in hot water till the skin will slip off them; pound them with a little orange flower or rose water, to keep them from oiling; mix with them four crackers, finely pounded, or two gills of rice flour; six eggs, a pint of cream, a pound of sugar, half a pound of butter, and four table-spoonsful of wine; put a nice paste in the bottom of your dish, garnish the edges, pour in the pudding, and bake it in a moderate oven

## QUIRE OF PAPER PANCAKES.

Beat sixteen eggs, add to them a quart of milk, a nutmeg, half a pound of flour, a pound of melted butter, a pound of sugar, and two gills of wine; take care the flour be not in lumps; butter the pan for the first pancake, run them as thin as possible, and when coloured, they are done; do not turn them, but lay them carefully in the dish, sprinkling powdered sugar between each layer—serve them up hot. This quantity will make four dozen pancakes.

---

## A CURD PUDDING.

Put two quarts of milk on the fire; when it boils, pour in half a pint of white wine, strain the curd from the whey, and pound it in a mortar, with six ounces of butter, half a pound of loaf sugar, and half a pint of rice flour, or as much crackers beaten as fine as flour; six eggs made light, and half a grated nutmeg— beat all well together, and bake them in saucers in a moderate oven; turn them out carefully in your dish, stick thin slices of citron in them, and pour on rich melted butter, with sugar and wine.

---

## LEMON PUDDING.

Grate the rind from six fresh lemons, squeeze the juice from three, and strain it; beat the yelks of six- teen eggs very light, put to them sixteen table-spoons- ful of powdered loaf sugar, not heaped up—the same of melted butter; add the grated rind, and the juice, with four crackers finely pounded, or an equal quantity

of rice flour; or for change, six ounces of **corn meal,**
which is excellent—beat it till light, put a puff **paste**
in your dish, pour the pudding in, and bake it in a
moderate oven—it must not be very brown.

## BREAD PUDDING.

GRATE the crumb of a stale loaf, and pour on it a
pint of boiling milk—let it stand an hour, then beat it
to a pulp; add six eggs, well beaten, half a pound of
butter, the same of powdered sugar, half a nutmeg,
a glass of brandy, and some grated lemon peel—put
a paste in the dish, and bake it.

## THE HENRIETTA PUDDING.

BEAT six eggs very light, sift into them a pound of
loaf sugar powdered, and a light pound of flour, with
half a grated nutmeg, and a glass of brandy; beat all
together very well, add a pint of cream, pour it in a
deep dish, and bake it—when done, sift some powdered sugar over it.

## TANSEY PUDDING.

BEAT seven eggs very light, mix with them a pint
of cream, and nearly as much spinach juice, with a
little juice of tansey; add a quarter of a pound of
powdered crackers or pounded rice made fine, a glass
of wine, some grated nutmeg and sugar; stir it over
the fire to thicken, pour it into a paste and bake it, or
fry it like an omelette.

## CHERRY PUDDING.

Beat six eggs very light, add half a pint of milk, six ounces flour, eight ounces grated bread, twelve ounces suet, chopped fine, a little salt; when it is beat well, mix in eighteen ounces preserved cherries or damsins; bake or boil it. Make a sauce of melted butter, sugar and wine.

## APPLE PIE.

Put a crust in the bottom of a dish, put on it a layer of ripe apples, pared and sliced thin—then a layer of powdered sugar; do this alternately till the dish is full; put in a few tea-spoonsful of rose water and some cloves—put on a crust and bake it.

## BAKED APPLE PUDDING.

Take well flavoured apples, bake, but do not burn them, rub them through a sieve, take one pound of the apples so prepared, mix with it, while hot, half a pound of butter, and half a pound of powdered sugar; the rinds of two lemons grated—and when cold, add six eggs well beaten; put a paste in the bottom of a dish, and pour in the apples—half an hour will bake it; sift a little sugar on the apples when baked.

## A NICE BOILED PUDDING.

Make up a pint of flour at sun rise, exactly as you do for bread; see that it rises well—have a large pot of water boiling; and half an hour before the puddings are to go to table, make the dough in balls, the size of a goose egg; throw them in the water, and boil them quickly, keeping the pot covered: they must be torn asunder, as cutting will make them heavy; eat them with powdered sugar, butter, and grated nutmeg.

## AN EXCELLENT AND CHEAP DESSERT DISH.

WASH a pint of small homony very clean, and boil it tender; add an equal quantity of corn meal, make it into a batter with eggs, milk, and a piece of butter; bake it like batter cakes on a griddle, and eat it with butter and molasses.

## SLICED APPLE PUDDING.

BEAT six eggs very light, add a pint of rich milk, pare some apples or peaches—slice them thin, make the eggs and milk into a tolerably thick batter with flour, add a small cup of melted butter, put in the fruit, and bake it in a deep dish—eat with sugar, butter, and nutmeg.

## BAKED INDIAN MEAL PUDDING.

BOIL one quart of milk, mix in it two gills and a half of corn meal very smoothly, seven eggs well beaten, a gill of molasses, and a good piece of butter; bake it two hours.

## BOILED INDIAN MEAL PUDDING

Mix one quart of corn meal, with three quarts of milk; take care it be not lumpy—add three eggs and a gill of molasses; it must be put on at sun rise, to eat at three o'clock; the great art in this pudding is tying the bag properly, as the meal swells very much.

## PUMPKIN PUDDING.

Stew a fine sweet pumpkin till soft and dry; rub it through a sieve, mix with the pulp six eggs quite light, a quarter of a pound of butter, half a pint of new milk, some pounded ginger and nutmeg, a wine glass of brandy, and sugar to your taste. Should it be too liquid, stew it a little drier, put a paste round the edges, and in the bottom of a shallow dish or plate—pour in the mixture, cut some thin bits of paste, twist them, and lay them across the top, and bake it nicely.

## FAYETTE PUDDING.

Slice a loaf of bread tolerably thick—lay the slices in the bottom of a dish, cutting them so as to cover it completely; sprinkle some sugar and nutmeg, with a little butter, on each layer; when all are in, pour on a quart of good boiled custard sweetened--serve it up cold.

## MACCARONI PUDDING.

Simmer half a pound of maccaroni in a plenty of water, with a table-spoonful of salt, till tender, but not broke—strain it, beat five yelks, two whites of eggs, half a pint of cream—mince white meat and boiled ham very fine, add three spoonsful of grated cheese, pepper and salt; mix these with the maccaroni, butter the mould, put it in, and steam it in a pan of boiling water for an hour—serve with rich gravy.

## POTATO PASTE.

Boil mealy potatos quite soft, first taking off the skins; rub them while hot through a sieve, put them in a stew pan over the fire, with as much water as will make it the consistence of thick mush; sift one quart of flour, and make it into a paste; with this mush, knead it till light, roll it out thin, make the dumplins small—fill them with apples, or any other fruit—tie them up in a thick cloth, and boil them nicely—eat them with butter, sugar, and nutmeg.

## COMPOTE OF APPLES.

Pare and core the apples, and if you prefer it, cut them in four, wash them clean, and put them in a pan with water and sugar enough to cover them; add cinnamon and lemon peel, which has been previously soaked, scraped on the inside, and cut in strings; boil them gently until the apples are done, take them out in a deep dish, boil the syrup to a proper consistency, and pour it on them: it will take a pound of sugar for a large dish.

## CHARLOTTE.

Stew any kind of fruit, and season it in any way you like best; soak some slices of bread in butter; put

them while hot, in the bottom and round the sides of
a dish, which has been rubbed with butter—put in
your fruit, and lay slices of bread prepared in the
same manner on the top: bake it a few minutes, turn
it carefully into another dish, sprinkle on some powdered sugar, and glaze it with a salamander.

## APPLE FRITTERS.

PARE some apples, and cut them in thin slices—put
them in a bowl, with a glass of brandy, some white
wine, a quarter of a pound of pounded sugar, a little
cinnamon finely powdered, and the rind of a lemon
grated; let them stand some time, turning them over
frequently; beat two eggs very light, add one quarter
of a pound of flour, a table-spoonful of melted butter,
and as much cold water as will make a thin batter;
drip the apples on a sieve, mix them with the batter,
take one slice with a spoonful of batter to each fritter,
fry them quickly of a light brown, drain them well,
put them in a dish, sprinkling sugar over each, and
glaze them nicely.

## BELL FRITTERS.

PUT a piece of butter the size of an egg into a pint
of water; let it boil a few minutes—thicken it very
smoothly with a pint of flour; let it remain a short
time on the fire, stir it all the time that it may not
stick to the pan, pour it in a wooden bowl, add five
or six eggs, breaking one and beating it in—then
another, and so on till they are all in, and the dough
quite light—put a pint of lard in a pan, let it boil.

make the fritters small, and fry them of a fine amber colour.

---

### BREAD FRITTERS.

Cut your bread of a convenient size, pour on it some white wine, and let it stand a few minutes—drain it on a sieve, beat four eggs very light, add four spoonsful of wine, beat all well together—have your lard boiling, dip the bread in the egg, and fry it a light brown; sprinkle sugar on each, and glaze them.

---

### SPANISH FRITTERS.

Make up a quart of flour, with one egg well beaten, a large spoonful of yeast, and as much milk as will make it a little softer than muffin dough; mix it early in the morning; when well risen, work in two spoonsful of melted butter, make it in balls the size of a walnut, and fry them a light brown in boiling lard - eat them with wine and sugar, or molasses.

---

### TO MAKE MUSH.

Put a lump of butter the size of an egg into a quart of water, make it sufficiently thick with corn meal and a little salt; it must be mixed perfectly smooth—stir it constantly till done enough.

---

# CAKES.

### JUMBALS.

Put one pound of nice sugar into two pounds of flour, add pounded spice of any kind, and pass them through a sieve; beat four eggs, pour them on with three quarters of a pound of melted butter, knead all well together, and bake them.

## MACAROONE.

Blanch a pound of sweet almonds, pound them in a mortar with rose water; whip the whites of seven eggs to a strong froth, put in one pound of powdered sugar, beat it some time, then put in the almonds—mix them well, and drop them on sheets of paper buttered; sift sugar over, and bake them quickly. Be careful not to let them get discoloured.

## TO MAKE DROP BISCUIT.

Beat eight eggs very light, add to them twelve ounces of flour, and one pound of sugar; when perfectly light, drop them on tin sheets, and bake them in a quick oven.

## TAVERN BISCUIT.

To one pound of flour, add half a pound of sugar, half a pound of butter, some mace and nutmeg powdered, and a glass of brandy or wine; wet it with milk, and when well kneaded, roll it thin, cut it in shapes, and bake it quickly.

## RUSK.

Rub half a pound of sugar into three pounds of flour—sift it, pour on half a pint of good yeast, beat six eggs, add half a pint of milk—mix all together, and knead it well: if not soft enough, add more milk—

it should be softer than bread; make it at night—in the morning, if well risen, work in six ounces of butter, and bake it in small rolls; when cold. slice it, lay it on tin sheets, and dry it in the oven.

### GINGER BREAD.

THREE quarts of flour, three quarters of a pound of brown sugar, a large spoonful of pounded ginger, one tea-spoonful of powdered cloves—sift it, melt half a pound of butter in a quart of rich molasses, wet the flour with it, knead it well, and bake it in a slack oven.

### PLEBEIAN GINGER BREAD.

MIX three large spoonsful of pounded ginger, with three quarts of flour—sift it, dissolve three tea-spoonsful of pearl-ash in a cup of water, and pour it on the flour; melt half a pound of butter in a quart of molasses, mix it with the flour, knead it well, cut it in shapes, and bake it.

### SUGAR GINGER BREAD.

TAKE two pounds of the nicest brown sugar, dry and pound it, put it into three quarts of flour, add a large cup full of powdered ginger, and sift the mixture; wash the salt out of a pound of butter, and cream it; have twelve eggs well beaten; work into the butter first, the mixture, then the froth from the eggs, until all are in, and it is quite light; add a glass of brandy butter snallow moulds, pour it in, and bake in a quick oven

## DOUGH NUTS—A YANKEE CAKE

Dry half a pound of good brown sugar, pound it and mix it with two pounds of flour, and sift it; add two spoonsful of yeast, and as much new milk as will make it like bread: when well risen, knead in half a pound of butter, make it in cakes the size of a half dollar, and fry them a light brown in boiling lard.

## RISEN CAKE.

Take three pounds of flour, one and a half of pounded sugar, a tea-spoonful of cloves, one of mace, and one of ginger, all finely powdered—pass the whole through a sieve, put to it four spoonsful of good yeast, and twelve eggs—mix it up well, and if not sufficiently soft, add a little milk: make it up at night, and set it to rise—when well risen, knead into it a pound of butter, and two gills of brandy; have ready two pounds of raisins stoned, mix all well together, pour it into a mould of proper size, and bake it in an oven heated as for bread; let it stand till thoroughly done, and do not take it from the* mould until quite cold.

## POUND CAKE.

Wash the salt from a pound of butter, and rub it till it is soft as cream—have ready a pound of flour sifted, one of powdered sugar, and twelve eggs well beaten; put alternately into the butter, sugar, flour, and the froth from the eggs—continuing to beat them together till all the ingredients are in, and the cake quite light: add some grated lemon peel, a nutmeg, and a gill of brandy; butter the pans, and bake them. This cake makes an excellent pudding, if baked in a large mould, and eaten with sugar and wine. It is also excellent when boiled, and served up with melted butter, sugar and wine.

## SAVOY OR SPUNGE CAKE.

TAKE twelve fresh eggs, put them in the scale, and balance them with sugar: take out half, and balance the other half with flour; separate the whites from the yelks, whip them up very light, then mix them, and sift in, first sugar, then flour, till both are exhausted; add some grated lemon peel; bake them in paper cases, or little tin moulds. This also makes an excellent pudding, with butter, sugar, and wine, for sauce.

## A RICH FRUIT CAKE.

HAVE the following articles prepared, before you begin the cake: four pounds of flour dried and sifted, four pounds of butter washed to free it from salt, two pounds of loaf sugar pounded, a quarter of a pound of mace, the same of nutmegs powdered; wash four pounds of currants clean, pick and dry them; blanch one pound of sweet almonds, and cut them in very thin slices; stone two pounds of raisins, cut them in two, and strew a little flour over to prevent their sticking together, and two pounds of citron sliced thin; break thirty eggs, separating the yelks and whites; work the butter to a cream with your hand—

put in alternately, flour, sugar, and the froth from both whites and yelks, which must be beaten separately, and *only* the froth put in.   When all are mixed and the cake looks very light, add the spice, with half a pint of brandy, the currants and almonds: butter the mould well, pour in part of the cake, strew over it some raisins and citron—do this until all is in: set it in a well heated oven: when it has risen, and the top is coloured, cover it with paper; it will require three hours baking—it must be iced.

### NAPLES BISCUIT

BEAT twelve eggs light, add to them one pound of flour, and one of powdered sugar; continue to beat all together till perfectly light; bake it in long pans, four inches wide, with divisions; so that each cake, when done, will be four inches long, and one and a half wide

### SHREWSBURY CAKES.

MIX a pound of sugar, with two pounds of flour, and a large spoonful of pounded coriander seeds; sift them, add three quarters of a pound of melted butter, six eggs, and a gill of brandy; knead it well, roll it thin, cut it in shapes, and bake without discolouring it.

### LITTLE PLUM CAKES.

PREPARE them as directed for pound cake, add raisins and currants, bake them in small tin shapes, and ice them.

## SODA CAKES

DISSOLVE half a pound of sugar in a pint of milk, add a tea-spoonful of soda; pour it on two pounds of flour—melt half a pound of butter, knead all together till light, put it in shallow moulds, and bake it quickly in a brisk oven.

---

## TO MAKE BREAD.

WHEN you find the barrel of flour a good one, empty it into a chest or box, made for the purpose, with a lid that will shut close: it keeps much better in this manner than when packed in a barrel, and even improves by lying lightly; sift the quantity you intend to make up—put into a bowl two gills and a half of water for each quart, with a tea-spoon heaped up with salt, and a large spoonful of yeast for each quart; stir this mixture well, put into another bowl one handful of flour from every quart; pour a little of the mixture on to wet it, then more, until you get it all in, taking great care that it be smooth, and quite free from lumps; beat it some minutes, take one-third of the flour out of the kettle, pour on the batter, and sprinkle over it the dry flour; stop the kettle, and set it where it can have a moderate degree of warmth: when it has risen well, turn it into a bowl, mix in the dry flour, and knead it on a board till it looks quite light; return it to the kettle, and place it where it can have proper heat: in the morning, take the dry crust carefully from the top, put the dough on a board, knead it well, make it into rolls, set them on tin sheets. put a towel over, and let them stand near the fire till the oven is ready. In winter, make the bread up at three o'clock, and it will be ready to work before bed time. In summer, make it up at five o'clock. A quart of flour should weigh just one pound and a quarter. The bread must be rasped when baked.

## TO MAKE NICE BISCUIT.

RUB a large spoonful of butter into a quart of risen dough, knead it well, and make it into biscuit, either thick or thin: bake them quickly.

## RICE BREAD.

BOIL six ounces of rice in a quart of water, till it is dry and soft—put it into two pounds of flour, mix it in well; add two tea-spoonsful of salt, two large spoonsful of yeast, and as much water as will make it the consistence of bread: when well risen, bake it in moulds.

## MIXED BREAD.

PUT a tea-spoonful of salt, and a large one of yeast, into a quart of flour; make it sufficiently soft, with corn meal gruel; when well risen, bake it in a mould. It is an excellent bread for breakfast. Indifferent flour will rise much better, when made with gruel. than with fair water.

## PATENT YEAST.

PUT half a pound of fresh hops into a gallon of water, and boil it away to two quarts; then strain it, and make it a thin batter with flour; add half a pint of good yeast, and when well fermented, pour it in a bowl, and work in as much corn meal as will make it the consistency of biscuit dough; set it to rise, and when quite light, make it into little cakes, which must be dried in the shade, turning them very frequently; keep them securely from damp and dust. Persons who live in town, and can procure brewer's yeast, will save trouble by using it: take one quart of it, add a quart of water, and proceed as before directed

## TO PREPARE THE CAKES.

TAKE one or more cakes, according to the flour you are to make; pour on a little warm water; when it is dissolved, stir it well, thicken with a little flour, and set it near the fire, to rise before it is used. The best thing to keep yeast in, is a small mug or pitcher, with a close stopper, under which must be placed a double fold of linen, to make it still closer. This is far preferable to a bottle, and more easily cleaned.

## ANOTHER METHOD FOR MAKING YEAST

PEEL one large Irish potato, boil it till soft, rub it through a sieve; add an equal quantity of flour, make it sufficiently liquid with hop tea; and when a little warmer than new milk, add a gill of good yeast; stir it well, and keep it closely covered in a small pitcher.

## NICE BUNS.

PUT four ounces of sugar with three quarters of a pound of flour; make it up with two spoonsful of yeast, and half a pint of milk; when well risen, work into it four ounces of butter, make it into small buns, and bake them in a quick oven—do not burn them.

## MUFFINS.

Sift a quart of flour, put to it a little salt, and a large spoonful of yeast—beat the white of a fresh egg to a strong froth, add it, and make the flour up with cold water, as soft as you can to allow it to be handled; set it in a moderately warm place. Next morning, beat it well with a spoon, put it on the griddle in a round form, and bake it nicely, turning them frequently till done.

## FRENCH ROLLS.

Sift a quart of flour, add a little salt, a spoonful of yeast, two eggs well beaten, and half a pint of milk—knead it, and set it to rise: next morning, work in an ounce of butter, make the dough into small rolls, and bake them. The top crust should not be hard.

## CRUMPETS.

Take a quart of dough from your bread at a very early hour in the morning; break three fresh eggs, separating the yelks from the whites—whip them both to a froth, mix them with the dough, and add gradually milk-warm water, till you make a batter the thickness of buckwheat cakes: beat it well, and set it to rise till near breakfast time; have the griddle ready, pour on the batter to look quite round: they do not require turning.

## APOQUINIMINC CAKES.

Put a little salt, one egg beaten, and four ounces of butter, in a quart of flour—make it into a paste with new milk, beat it for half an hour with a pestle, roll the paste thin, and cut it into round cakes; bake them on a gridiron, and be careful not to burn them.

## BATTER CAKES.

BOIL two cups of small homony very soft; add an equal quantity of corn meal with a little salt, and a large spoonful of butter; make it in a thin batter with three eggs, and a sufficient quantity of milk—beat all together some time, and bake them on a griddle, or in woffle irons. When eggs cannot be procured, yeast makes a good substitute; put a spoonful in the batter, and let it stand an hour to rise.

## BATTER BREAD.

TAKE six spoonsful of flour and three of corn meal, with a little salt—sift them, and make a thin batter with four eggs, and a sufficient quantity of rich milk; bake it in little tin moulds in a quick oven.

## CREAM CAKES.

MELT as much butter in a pint of milk, as will make it rich as cream—make the flour into a paste with this, knead it well, roll it out frequently, cut it in squares, and bake on a griddle.

## SOUFLE BISCUITS.

RUB four ounces of butter into a quart of flour, make it into paste with milk, knead it well, roll it as thin as paper, and bake it to look white

## CORN MEAL BREAD.

Rub a piece of butter the size of an egg, into a pint of corn meal—make it a batter with two eggs, and some new milk—add a spoonful of yeast, set it by the fire an hour to rise, butter little pans, and bake it.

## SWEET POTATO BUNS.

Boil and mash a potato, rub into it as much flour as will make it like bread—add spice and sugar to your taste, with a spoonful of yeast; when it has risen well, work in a piece of butter, bake it in small rolls, to be eaten hot with butter, either for breakfast or tea.

## RICE WOFFLES.

Boil two gills of rice quite soft, mix with it three gills of flour, a little salt, two ounces melted butter, two eggs beaten well, and as much milk as will make it a thick batter—beat it till very light, and bake it in woffle irons.

## VELVET CAKES.

Make a batter of one quart of flour, three eggs, a quart of milk, and a gill of yeast; when well risen, stir in a large spoonful of melted butter, and bake them in muffin hoops.

## CHOCOLATE CAKES.

Put half a pound of nice brown sugar into a quart of flour, sift it, and make it into a paste, with four ounces of butter melted in as much milk as will wet it; knead it till light, roll it tolerably thin, cut it in strips an inch wide, and just long enough to lay in a plate; bake them on a griddle, put them in the plate in rows to checker each other, and serve them to eat with chocolate.

---

### WAFERS.

BEAT six eggs, add a pint of flour, two ounces of melted butter, with as much milk as will make a thin batter—put in pounded loaf sugar to your taste, pour it in the wafer irons, bake them quickly without browning, and roll them while hot.

---

### BUCKWHEAT CAKES.

PUT a large spoonful of yeast and a little salt, into a quart of buckwheat meal; make it into a batter with cold water; let it rise well, and bake it on a griddle— it turns sour very quickly, if it be allowed to stand any time after it has risen.

---

### OBSERVATIONS ON ICE CREAMS.

IT is the practice with some indolent cooks, to set the freezer containing the cream, in a tub with ice and salt, and put it in the ice house; it will certainly freeze there; but not until the watery particles have subsided, and by the separation destroyed the cream. A freezer should be twelve or fourteen inches deep, and eight or ten wide. This facilitates the operation very much, by giving a larger surface for the ice to form, which it always does on the sides of the vessel; a silver spoon with a long handle should be provided for scraping the ice from the sides as soon as formed:

and when the whole is congealed, pack it in moulds (which must be placed with care, lest they should not be upright,) in ice and salt, till sufficiently hard to retain the shape—they should not be turned out till the moment they are to be served. The freezing tub must be wide enough to leave a margin of four or five inches all around the freezer, when placed in the middle—which must be filled up with small lumps of ice mixed with salt—a larger tub would waste the ice. The freezer must be kept constantly in motion during the process, and ought to be made of pewter, which is less liable than tin to be worn in holes, and spoil the cream by admitting the salt water.

## ICE CREAMS.

WHEN ice creams are not put into shapes, they should always be served in glasses with handles.

## VANILLA CREAM.

BOIL a Vanilla bean in a quart of rich milk, until it has imparted the flavour sufficiently—then take it out, and mix with the milk, eight eggs, yelks and whites beaten well; let it boil a little longer; make it very sweet, for much of the sugar is lost in the operation of freezing.

## RASPBERRY CREAM.

MAKE a quart of rich boiled custard—when cold, pour it on a quart of ripe red raspberries; mash them in it, pass it through a sieve, sweeten, and freeze it

### STRAWBERRY CREAM

Is made in the same manner—the strawberries must be very ripe, and the stems picked out. If rich cream can be procured, it will be infinitely better—the custard is intended as a substitute, when cream cannot be had.

---

### COCOA NUT CREAM.

Take the nut from its shell, pare it, and grate it very fine; mix it with a quart of cream, sweeten, and freeze it. If the nut be a small one, it will require one and a half to flavour a quart of cream.

---

### CHOCOLATE CREAM.

Scrape a quarter of a pound of chocolate very fine, put it in a quart of milk, boil it till the chocolate is dissolved, stirring it continually—thicken with six eggs. A Vanilla bean boiled with the milk, will improve the flavour greatly.

---

### OYSTER CREAM.

Make a rich soup, (see directions for oyster soup,) strain it from the oysters, and freeze it.

---

### ICED JELLY.

Make calf's foot jelly not very stiff, freeze it, and serve it in glasses.

---

### PEACH CREAM.

Get fine soft peaches perfectly ripe, peel them, take out the stones, and put them in a China bowl:

sprinkle some sugar on, and chop them very small with a silver spoon—if the peaches be sufficiently ripe, they will become a smooth pulp; add as much cream or rich milk as you have peaches; put more sugar, and freeze it.

## COFFEE CREAM.

Toast two gills of raw coffee till it is a light brown, and not a grain burnt; put it hot from the toaster without grinding it, into a quart of rich, and perfectly sweet milk; boil it, and add the yelks of eight eggs; when done, strain it through a sieve, and sweeten it; if properly done, it will not be discoloured. The coffee may be dried, and will answer for making in the usual way to drink, allowing more for the quantity of water, than if it had not gone through this process.

## QUINCE CREAM.

Wash ripe quinces and boil them whole till quite tender—let them stand to drain and cool—then rub them through a hair sieve; mix with the pulp as much cochineal finely powdered, as will make it a pretty colour; then add an equal quantity of cream, and sweeten it. Pears or apples may be used, prepared in the same manner.

## CITRON CREAM.

Cut the finest citron melons when perfectly ripe—take out the seeds, and slice the nicest part into a China bowl in small pieces, that will lie conveniently; cover them with powdered sugar, and let them stand several hours—then drain off the syrup they have made, and add as much cream as it will give a **strong** flavour to, and freeze it. Pine apples may be used in the same way.

---

## ALMOND CREAM.

Pour hot water on the almonds, and let them stand till the skins will slip off, then pound them fine, and mix them with cream: a pound of almonds in the shells, will be sufficient for a quart of cream—sweeten and freeze it. The kernels of the common black walnut, prepared in the same way, make an excellent cream.

---

## LEMON CREAM.

Pare the yellow rind very thin from four lemons— put them in a quart of fresh cream, and boil it; squeeze and strain the juice of one lemon, saturate it completely with powdered sugar; and when the cream is quite cold, stir it in—take care that it does not curdle—if not sufficiently sweet, add more sugar.

---

## LEMONADE ICED.

Make a quart of rich lemonade, whip the whites of six fresh eggs to a strong froth—mix them well with the lemonade, and freeze it. The juice of morello cher ries, or of currants mixed with water and sugar, and prepared in the same way, make very delicate ices.

---

## TO MAKE CUSTARD.

Make a quart of milk quite hot, that it may not whey when baked; let it stand to get cold, and then mix six eggs with it; sweeten it with loaf sugar, and fill the custard cups—put on the covers, and set them in a Dutch oven with water, but not enough to risk its boiling into the cups; do not put on the top of the oven. When the water has boiled ten or fifteen minutes, take out a cup, and if the custard be the consistence of jelly, it is sufficiently done; serve them in the cups with the covers on, and a tea-spoon on the dish between each cup—grate nutmeg on the tops when cold.

## TO MAKE A TRIFLE.

PUT slices of Savoy cake or Naples biscuit at the bottom of a deep dish; wet it with white wine, and fill the dish nearly to the top with rich boiled custard; season half a pint of cream with white wine and sugar; whip it to a froth—as it rises, take it lightly off, and lay it on the custard; pile it up high and tastily—decorate it with preserves of any kind, cut so thin as not to bear the froth down by its weight.

## RICE BLANC MANGE.

BOIL a tea-cup full of rice in a very small quantity of water, till it is near bursting—then add half a pint of milk, boil it to a mush, stirring all the time; season it with sugar, wine, and nutmeg; dip the mould in water, and fill it; when cold, turn it in a dish, and surround it with boiled custard seasoned, or syllabub—garnish it with marmalade.

## FLOATING ISLAND

HAVE the bowl nearly full of syllabub, made with milk, white wine, and sugar; beat the whites of six

new laid eggs to a strong froth—then mix with it raspberry or strawberry marmalade enough to flavour and
colour it; lay the froth lightly on the syllabub, first
putting in some slices of cake; raise it in little mounds,
and garnish with something light.

### SYLLABUB.

SEASON the milk with sugar and white wine, but not
enough to curdle it; fill the glasses nearly full, and
crown them with whipt cream seasoned.

# COLD CREAMS.

### LEMON CREAM.

PARE the rind very thin from four fresh lemons,
squeeze the juice, and strain it—put them both into
a quart of water, sweeten it to your taste, add the
whites of six eggs, beat to a froth; set it over the fire,
and keep stirring until it thickens, but do not let it
boil—then pour it in a bowl; when cold, strain it
through a sieve, put it on the fire, and add the yelks
of the eggs—stir it till quite thick, and serve it in
glasses.

### ORANGE CREAM

Is made in the same manner, but requires more juice
to give a flavour.

### RASPBERRY CREAM.

STIR as much raspberry marmalade into a quart of
cream, as will be sufficient to give a rich flavour of

the fruit—strain it, and fill your glasses, leaving out a part to whip into froth for the top.

## TEA CREAM.

Put one ounce of the best tea in a pitcher, pour on it a table spoonful of water, and let it stand an hour to soften the leaves; then put to it a quart of boiling cream, cover it close, and in half an hour strain it; add four tea-spoonsful of a strong infusion of rennet in water, stir it, and set it on some hot ashes, and cover it; when you find by cooling a little of it, that it will jelly, pour it into glasses, and garnish with thin bits of preserved fruit.

## SAGO CREAM.

Wash the sago clean, and put it on the fire with a stick of cinnamon, and as much water as will boil it thick and soft; take out the cinnamon, and add rich boiled custard till it is of a proper thickness; sweeten it, and serve in glasses or cups, with grated nutmeg on the top.

## BARLEY CREAM

Is made the same way—you may add a little white wine to both; it will give an agreeable flavour.

## GOOSEBERRY FOOL.

Pick the stems and blossoms from two quarts of green gooseberries; put them in a stew pan, with their weight in loaf sugar, and a very little water—when sufficiently stewed, pass the pulp through a sieve; and

when cold, add rich boiled custard till it is like thick
cream; put it in a glass bowl, and lay frothed cream
on the top.

## TO MAKE SLIP.

`Make a quart of rich milk moderately warm: then
stir into it one large spoonful of the preparation of rennet, (see receipt to prepare rennet,) set it by, and
when cold, it will be as stiff as jelly. It should be
made only a few hours before it is used, or it will be
tough and watery; in summer, set the dish in ice after
it has jellied—it must be eaten with powdered sugar,
cream, and nutmeg.

## CURDS AND CREAM.

Turn one quart of milk as for the slip—let it stand
until just before it is to be served: then take it up with
a skimming dish, and lay it on a sieve—when the
whey has drained off, put the curds in a dish, and
surround them with cream—use sugar and nutmeg.
These are Arcadian dishes; very delicious, cheap, and
easily prepared.

## BLANC MANGE.

Break one ounce of isinglass into very small pieces;
wash it well, and pour on a pint of boiling water; next
morning, add a quart of milk, boil it till the isinglass is
dissolved, strain it, put in two ounces sweet almonds,
blanched and pounded; sweeten it, and put it in the
mould—when stiff, turn them into a deep dish, and
put raspberry cream around them. For a change, stick
thin slips of blanched almonds all over the blanc mange.

and dress round with syllabub, nicely frothed. Some moulds require colouring—for an ear of corn, mix the yelk of an egg with a little of the blanc mange; fill the grains of the corn with it—and when quite set, pour in the white, but take care it is not warm enough to melt the yellow: for a bunch of asparagus, colour a little with spinach juice, to fill the green tops of the heads. Fruit must be made the natural colour of what it represents. Cochineal and alkanet root pounded and dissolved in brandy, make good colouring; but blanc mange should never be served, without raspberry cream or syllabub to eat with it.

## TO MAKE A HEN'S NEST.

GET five small eggs, make a hole at one end, and empty the shells—fill them with blanc mange: when stiff and cold, take off the shells, pare the yellow rind very thin from six lemons, boil them in water till tender, then cut them in thin strips to resemble straw, and preserve them with sugar; fill a small deep dish half full of nice jelly—when it is set, put the straw on in form of a nest, and lay the eggs in it. It is a beautiful dish for a dessert or supper.

### Little Dishes for a Second Course, or Supper.

## PHEASANTS A-LA-DAUB.

ROAST two pheasants in the nicest manner—get a deep dish, the size and form of the one you intend to serve the pheasants in—it must be as deep as a tureen; put in savoury jelly about an inch and a half at the bottom; when that is set, and the pheasants cold, lay

them on the jelly with their breasts down; fill the dish
with jelly up to their backs; take care it is not warm
enough to melt the other, and that the birds are not
displaced—just before it is to be served, set it a moment in hot water to loosen it; put the dish on the top,
and turn it out carefully.

## PARTRIDGES A-LA-DAUB.

Truss six partridges neatly, cover them with thin
slices of fat bacon taken from the top of a middling;
this keeps them white, and gives a good flavour; they
must be wrapped entirely in it—roast them, and when
done, take off the bacon; let them get cold, and use
jelly as for the pheasants.

## CHICKENS A-LA-DAUB.

Roast two half grown chickens, cut off the legs
and wings, pull the breast from each side entire, take
the skin from all the pieces, lay it in the dish, and
cover it with jelly.

## TO MAKE SAVOURY JELLY.

Put eight or ten pounds of coarse lean beef, or the
same quantity of the inferior parts of the fore quarter
of veal, into a pot with two gallons of water, a pound
of lean salt pork, three large onions chopped, three
carrots, a large handful of parsley, and any sweet
herb that you choose, with pepper and salt; boil it
very gently till reduced to two quarts; strain it through
a sieve—next day, take off the fat, turn out the jelly,
and separate it from the dregs at the bottom; put it on
the fire with half a pint of white wine, a large spoon-

ful of lemon pickle, and the whites and shells of four eggs beaten: when it boils clear on one side, run it through the jelly bag.

---

## TURKEY A-LA-DAUB.

BONE a small turkey, put pepper and salt on the inside, and cover it with slices of boiled ham or tongue; fill it with well seasoned forcemeat, sew it up and boil it—cover it with jelly.

---

## SALMAGUNDI.

TURN a bowl on the dish, and put on it in regular rings, beginning at the bottom, the following ingredients, all minced:—anchovies with the bones taken out, the white meat of fowls without the skin, hard boiled eggs, the yelks and whites chopped separately, parsley, the lean of old ham scraped, the inner stalks of celery; put a row of capers round the bottom of the bowl, and dispose the others in a fanciful manner; put a little pyramid of butter on the top, and have a small glass with egg mixed as for sallad, to eat with the salmagundi.

---

## AN EXCELLENT RELISH AFTER DINNER.

PUT some soup or gravy from any of the dishes on the table, into the stew dish; add a good portion of pepper, vinegar, wine, catsup and salt; let it be very highly seasoned; broil the legs, liver, and gizzard of a turkey, the kidney of veal, or any thing you fancy; cut it up in small pieces: when broiled, put it in the gravy, and stew it at table.

## TO STEW PERCH.

LAY the perch in a deep pan with the heads on; sprinkle salt, pepper, and a little chopped onion over each layer; when they are all in, take as much water as will be sufficient to fill the pan less than half full; add a gill of wine, one of catsup, a little lemon pickle and spice; cover the pan, and let it stew gently till done; take out the fish without breaking, put them in a deep dish, pour the gravy on, and neatly turn them out.

# PRESERVES.

### DIRECTIONS FOR MAKING PRESERVES.

THE preserving pan should be made of bell metal, flat at the bottom, very large in diameter, but not deep. It should have a cover to fit closely, and handles at the sides of the pan, for taking it off with ease when the syrup boils too fast. There should also be a large chafing-dish with long legs, for the convenience of moving it to any part of the room. The process is a tedious one; and if the superintendent be not comfortably situated, the preserves cannot be properly managed. A ladle the size of a saucer, pierced and having a long handle, will be necessary for taking up the fruit without syrup. When a chafing-dish cannot be procured, the best substitute is a brick stove, with a grating, to burn charcoal. The sugar should be the best double refined; but if the pure amber coloured sugar house syrup from the West Indies can be got, it is greatly superior; it never ferments, and the trouble is very much lessened by having ready made syrup, in which it is only necessary to boil the fruit till clear. All delicate fruit should be done gently, and not allowed to remain more than half an hour after it begins to stew, before it is laid on dishes to cool; it must be put into the syrup again for the same time; continue this until it is sufficiently transparent. The advantage of this method is that the preserves are less liable to boil to pieces, than when done all at one time. It is injudicious to put more in the pan at once, than can lie on the bottom without crowding. The pan must be made bright, and nothing permitted to cool in it, lest it should canker. Delicate preserves should be kept in small glasses or pots, that will not hold more than one or two pounds, for the admission of air injures them; put letter paper wet with brandy on the preserves, and cover the tops with many folds of soft paper, that will tie round closely; keep them in a dry place, and expose them constantly to the sun to check fermentation. Fruit for preserving should be in full perfection, but not too ripe.

## TO PRESERVE CLING-STONE PEACHES.

Get the finest yellow cling-stones, pare them, and lay them in a bowl; have their weight of sugar pounded, and sprinkle it over them as they are put in; let them stand two or three hours, put them together with the sugar into the pan, add a little water, and let the peaches remain till thoroughly scalded; take them out with the ladle, draining off the syrup; should there not be enough to cover the peaches, add more water, boil it and skim it, return the fruit, and do them gently till quite clear. Have some stones cracked, blanch the kernels, and preserve them with the peaches.

## CLING-STONES SLICED.

PARE the peaches, and cut them in as large slices as possible; have their weight in sugar, and preserve them as the others.

---

## SOFT PEACHES.

GET yellow soft peaches that are not quite ripe, pare and divide them, scrape the places where the stones lay with a tea-spoon, and follow the former directions.

---

## PEACH MARMALADE.

TAKE the ripest soft peaches, (the yellow ones make the prettiest marmalade,) pare them, and take out the stones; put them in the pan with one pound of dry light coloured brown sugar to two of peaches: when they are juicy, they do not require water: with a silver or wooden spoon, chop them with the sugar; continue to do this, and let them boil gently till they are a transparent pulp, that will be a jelly when cold. Puffs made of this marmalade are very delicious.

---

## PEACH CHIPS.

SLICE them thin, and boil them till clear in a syrup made with half their weight of sugar; lay them on dishes in the sun, and turn them till dry; pack them in pots with powdered sugar sifted over each layer; should there be syrup left, continue the process with other peaches. They are very nice when done with pure honey instead of sugar.

## PEARS.

THE small pears are better for preserving than large ones. Pare them, and make a syrup, with their weight of sugar, and a little water—leave the stem on, and stick a clove in the blossom end of each; stew them till perfectly transparent.

## PEAR MARMALADE.

BOIL the pears till soft—when cold, rub the pulp through a sieve, and boil it to a jelly, allowing one pound of sugar to two of pears.

## QUINCES.

SELECT the finest and most perfect quinces, lay them on shelves, but do not let them touch each other; keep them till they look yellow and have a fragrant smell; put as many in the preserving pan as can lie conveniently, cover them with water, and scald them well: then take out the cores, and put them in water; cover the pan and boil them some time; strain the water, add to it the weight of the quinces in pounded loaf sugar, dissolve and skim it, pare the quinces, put them in the pan, and should there not be syrup enough to cover them, add more water—stew them till quite transparent. They will be light coloured if kept covered during the process, and red if the cover be taken off. Fill the space the cores occupied with quince jelly, before they are put into the pots—and cover them with syrup.

## CURRANT JELLY.

PICK full ripe currants from the stem, and put them in a stone pot; then set it in an iron pot of water—take care that no water gets in: when the currants have yielded their juice, pour them into a jelly bag—let it run as long as it will without pressing, which must be reserved for the best jelly; you may then squeeze the bag to make inferior kind. To each pint of this juice, put one pound of loaf sugar powdered—boil it fifteen or twenty minutes—skim it clean, and put it in glasses; expose them daily to the sun to prevent fermentation.

## QUINCE JELLY.

PREPARE the quinces as before directed, take off the stems and blossoms, wash them clean, and cut them in slices without paring; fill the pan, and pour in water to cover them—stew them gently, putting in a little water occasionally till they are soft; then pour them into a jelly bag; let all the liquor run through without pressing it, which must be set aside for the best jelly; to each pint of this, put a pound of loaf sugar pounded, and boil it to a jelly. The bag may be squeezed for an inferior, but a very nice jelly.

## QUINCE MARMALADE.

BOIL the quinces in water until soft, let them cool, and rub all the pulp through a sieve: put two pounds of it to one of sugar, pound a little cochineal, sift it through fine muslin, and mix it with the quince to give a colour; pick out the seeds, tie them in a muslin bag, and boil them with the marmalade: when it is a thick jelly, take out the seeds, and put it in pots.

## CHERRIES.

THE most beautiful cherries to preserve, are the carnation and common light red, with short stems; select the finest that are not too ripe; take an equal weight with the cherries of double refined sugar, make it into a syrup, and preserve them without stoning, and with the stems on; if they be done carefully, and the "Directions for preserving" closely attended to, the stems will not come off, and they will be so transparent that the stones may be seen.

## MORELLO CHERRIES.

TAKE out the stones with a quill over a deep dish, to save the juice that runs from them; put to the juice a pound of sugar for each pound of cherries, weighed after they are stoned; boil and skim the syrup, then put in the fruit, and stew till quite clear.

## TO DRY CHERRIES.

STONE them, and save the juice: weigh the cherries, and allow one pound of good brown sugar to three of the fruit; boil it with the juice, put the cherries in, stew them fifteen or twenty minutes, take them out, drain off the syrup, and lay the cherries in dishes to dry in the sun; keep the syrup to pour over a little at a time, as it dries on the cherries, which must be frequently turned over; when all the syrup is used, put the cherries away in pots, sprinkling a little powdered loaf sugar between the layers. They make excellent pies, puddings, and charlottes.

### RASPBERRY JAM.

To each pound of ripe red or English raspberries, put one pound of loaf sugar—stir it frequently, and stew till it is a thick jelly.

### TO PRESERVE STRAWBERRIES.

GET the largest strawberries before they are too ripe; have the best loaf sugar, one pound to each of strawberries—stew them very gently, taking them out to cool frequently, that they may not be mashed; when they look clear, they are done enough.

### STRAWBERRY JAM

Is made in the same manner as the raspberry, and is very fine to mix with cream for blanc mange, puffs, sweetmeat puddings, &c. &c.

### GOOSEBERRIES.

SELECT young gooseberries, make a syrup with one pound of loaf sugar to each of fruit; stew them till quite clear and the syrup becomes thick, but do not let them be mashed. They are excellent made into tarts—do not cover the pan while they are stewing.

### APRICOTS IN BRANDY.

TAKE freshly gathered apricots not too ripe; to half their weight of loaf sugar, add as much water as will cover the fruit; boil and skim it: then put in the apricots, and let them remain five or six minutes: take them up without syrup, and lay them on dishes to cool; boil the syrup till reduced one half; when the apricots are cold, put them in bottles, and cover then with equal quantities of syrup and French brandy. If the apricots be cling-stones, they will require more scalding.

## PEACHES IN BRANDY.

GET yellow soft peaches, perfectly free from defect and newly gathered, but not too ripe; place them in a pot, and cover them with cold weak lye; turn over those that float frequently, that the lye may act equally on them; at the end of an hour take them out, wipe them carefully with a soft cloth to get off the down and skin, and lay them in cold water; make a syrup as for the apricots, and proceed in the same manner, only scald the peaches more.

## CHERRIES IN BRANDY.

GET the short stemmed bright red cherries in bunches—make a syrup, with equal quantities of sugar and cherries; scald the cherries, but do not let the skins crack, which they will do if the fruit be too ripe.

## MAGNUM BONUM PLUMS IN BRANDY.

SELECT those that are free from blemish—make a syrup with half their weight of sugar, and preserve them in the same manner directed for apricots—green gages. The large amber, and the blue plums, are also excellent, done in the same way.

# PICKLING.

### LEMON PICKLE.

GRATE the yellow rind from two dozen fine fresh lemons, quarter them but leave them whole at the bottom; sprinkle salt on them, and put them in the sun every day until dry; then brush off the salt, put them in a pot with one ounce of nutmegs, and one of mace pounded; a large handful of horse radish scraped and dried two dozen cloves of garlic, and a pint of mustard seed; pour on one gallon of strong vinegar, tie the pot close, put a board on, and let it stand three months—strain it, and when perfectly clear, bottle it.

## TOMATO CATSUP.

Gather a peck of tomatos, pick out the stems, and wash them; put them on the fire without water, sprinkle on a few spoonsful of salt, let them boil steadily an hour, stirring them frequently; strain them through a colander, and then through a sieve; put the liquid on the fire with half a pint of chopped onions, half a quarter of an ounce of mace broke into small pieces; and if not sufficiently salt, add a little more—one table-spoonful of whole black pepper; boil all together until just enough to fill two bottles; cork it tight. Make it in August, in dry weather.

## TOMATO MARMALADE.

Gather full grown tomatos while quite green; take out the stems, and stew them till soft; rub them through a sieve, put the pulp on the fire seasoned highly with pepper, salt, and pounded cloves; add some garlic, and stew all together till thick: it keeps well, and is excellent for seasoning gravies. &c. &c.

## TOMATO SWEET MARMALADE.

Prepare it in the same manner, mix some loaf sugar with the pulp, and stew until it is a stiff jelly.

## TOMATO SOY.

TAKE a bushel of full ripe tomatos, cut them in slices without skinning—sprinkle the bottom of a large tub with salt, strew in the tomatos, and over each layer of about two inches thick, sprinkle half a pint of salt, and three onions sliced without taking off the skins.

When the bushel of tomatos is thus prepared, let them remain for *three* days, then put them into a large iron pot, in which they must boil from early in the morning till night, constantly stirring to prevent their sticking and mashing them.

The next morning, pass the mixture through a sieve, pressing it to obtain all the liquor you can; and add to it one ounce of cloves, quarter of a pound of allspice, quarter of a pound of whole black pepper, and a small wine glass of Cayenne; let it boil slowly and constantly during the whole of the day—in the evening, put it into a suitable vessel to cool; and the day after, bottle and cork it well: place it in a cool situation during warm weather, and it will keep for many years, provided it has been boiled very slowly and sufficiently in the preparation. Should it ferment it must be boiled a second time.

## PEPPER VINEGAR.

GET one dozen pods of pepper when ripe, take out the stems, and cut them in two; put them in a kettle with three pints of vinegar, boil it away to one quart, and strain it through a sieve. A little of this is excellent in gravy of every kind, and gives a flavour greatly superior to black pepper; it is also very fine when added to each of the various catsups for fish sauce.

## MUSHROOM CATSUP.

TAKE the flaps of the proper mushrooms from the stems—wash them, add some salt, and crush them; then boil them some time, strain them through a cloth, put them on the fire again with salt to your taste, a few cloves of garlic, and a quarter of an ounce of cloves pounded, to a peck of mushrooms; boil it till reduced to less than half the original quantity—bottle and cork it well.

## TARRAGON OR ASTRAGON VINEGAR.

PICK the tarragon nicely from the stem, let it lie in a dry place forty-eight hours; put it in a pitcher, and to one quart of the leaves put three pints of strong vinegar; cover it close, and let it stand a week—then strain it, and after standing in the pitcher till quite clear, bottle it, and cork it closely.

## CURRY POWDER.

ONE ounce turmeric, one do. coriander seed, one do. cummin seed, one do. white ginger, one of nutmeg, one of mace, and one of Cayenne pepper; pound all together, and pass them through a fine sieve; bottle and cork it well—one tea-spoonful is sufficient to season any made dish.

## TO PICKLE CUCUMBERS.

GATHER them full grown, but quite young—take off the green rind, and slice them tolerably thick; put a layer in a deep dish, strew over it some chopped onion and salt; do this until they are all in; sprinkle salt on the top, let them stand six hours, put them in a colan der—when all the liquor has run off, put them in a pot. strew a little cayenne pepper over each layer, and cover them with strong cold vinegar; when the pot is full, pour on some sweet oil, and tie it up close; at the end of a fortnight, pour off the first vinegar, and put on fresh.

---

## OIL MANGOS.

GATHER the melons a size larger than a goose egg—put them in a pot, pour boiling salt and water made strong upon them, and cover them up; next day, cut a slit from the stem to the blossom end, and take out the seeds carefully—return them to the brine, and let them remain in it eight days; then put them in strong vinegar for a fortnight, wipe the insides with a soft cloth, stuff them and tie them, pack them in a pot with the slit uppermost; strew some of the stuffing over each layer, and keep them covered with the best vinegar.

---

## TO MAKE THE STUFFING FOR FORTY MELONS.

WASH a pound of white race ginger very clean; pour boiling water on it, and let it stand twenty-four hours; slice it thin, and dry it; one pound of horse-radish scraped and dried, one pound of mustard seed washed and dried, one pound of chopped onion, one ounce of mace, one of nutmeg pounded fine, two ounces of turmeric, and a handful of whole black pepper; make these ingredients into a paste, with a quarter of a pound of mustard, and a large cup full of sweet oil; put a clove of garlic into each mango

## TO MAKE YELLOW PICKLE.

Put all the articles intended for the yellow pickle in a pot, and pour on them boiling salt and water—let them stand forty-eight hours, take advantage of a clear hot day, press the water from the articles, and lay them to dry in full sunshine, on a table covered with a thick soft cloth, with the corners pinned securely, that they may not blow up over the things—the cloth absorbs the moisture; and by turning them frequently on a dry place, they become white, and receive the colour of the turmeric more readily—one day of clear sunshine is enough to prepare them for the first vinegar.  When dried, put them in a pot of plain cold vinegar, with a little turmeric in it—let them remain in it two weeks to draw off the water from them, and to make them plump—then put them in a clean pot, and pour on the vinegar, prepared by the following directions—this is the most economical and best way of keeping them—mix the turmeric very smoothly, before you add it to your pickles.

## TO MAKE GREEN PICKLES.

Put the articles you intend to pickle, in a pot—and cover them with boiling salt and water: put a thick cloth on the top, and then a plate that will fit it—let it stand till the next morning, then pour off the salt and water, boil it again, and cover them as before; do this until your pickles are a good green—then put them in plain cold vinegar, with some turmeric in it; and at the end of a fortnight, put them up, as you do the yellow pickle.

## TO PREPARE VINEGAR FOR GREEN OR YELLOW PICKLE.

ONE pound of ginger sliced and dried, one of horse-radish scraped and dried, one of mustard seed washed and dried, one ounce long pepper, an ounce of mace, and one of nutmegs finely pounded; put all these ingredients in a pot, pour two gallons of strong vinegar on, and let it stand twelve months, stirring it very frequently. When this vinegar is used for the pickles, put two gallons more vinegar, with some mace and nutmegs, and keep it for another year. When the prepared vinegar is poured from the ingredients, do it very carefully, that it may be quite clear. Pickles keep much better when the vinegar is not boiled. Should the green pickles at any time lose their colour, it may be restored by adding a little more turmeric. All pickles are best, when one or two years old.

## TO PICKLE ONIONS.

GET white onions that are not too large, cut the stem close to the root with a sharp knife, put them in a pot, pour on boiling salt and water to cover them, stop the pot closely, let them stand a fortnight, changing the salt and water every three days; they must be stirred daily, or those that float will become soft; at the end of this time, take off the skin and outer shell, put them in plain cold vinegar with a little turmeric. If the vinegar be not very pale, the onion will not be of a good colour.

## TO PICKLE NASTERTIUMS.

GATHER the berries when full grown but young, put them in a pot, pour boiling salt and water on, and et them stand three or four days; then drain off the water, and cover them with cold vinegar; add a few blades of mace, and whole grains of black pepper.

## TO PICKLE RADISH PODS.

Cut them in nice bunches as soon as they are fully formed; they must be young and tender—pour boiling salt and water on them, cover with a thick cloth, and pewter plate, to keep in the steam; repeat this every day till they are a good green; then put them in cold vinegar, with mace and whole pepper; mix a little turmeric, with a small portion of oil, and stir it into the vinegar; it will make the pods of a more lively green. They are very pretty for garnishing meats

## TO PICKLE ENGLISH WALNUTS.

The walnuts should be gathered when the nut is so young that you can run a pin into it easily; pour boiling salt and water on, and let them be covered with it nine days, changing it every third day—take them out, and put them on dishes in the air for a few minutes, taking care to turn them over; this will make them black much sooner—put them in a pot, strew over some whole pepper, cloves, a little garlic, mustard seed, and horse-radish scraped and dried; cover them with strong cold vinegar.

## TO PICKLE PEPPERS.

Gather the large bell pepper when quite young, leave the seeds in and the stem on, cut a slit in one side between the large veins, to let the water in; pour boiling salt and water on, changing it every day for three weeks—you must keep them closely stopped; if,

at the end of this time, they be a good green, put them
in pots, and cover them with cold vinegar and a little
turmeric; those that are not sufficiently green, must be
continued under the same process till they are so   Be
careful not to cut through the large veins, as the heat
will instantly diffuse itself through the pod.

## TO MAKE WALNUT CATSUP.

GATHER the walnuts as for pickling, and keep them
in salt and water the same time; then pound them in
a marble mortar—to every dozen walnuts, put a quart
of vinegar; stir them well every day for a week, then
put them in a bag, and press all the liquor through;
to each quart, put a tea-spoonful of pounded cloves,
and one of mace, with six cloves of garlic—boil it
fifteen or twenty minutes, and bottle it.

## TO PICKLE GREEN NECTARINES OR APRI-COTS.

GATHER them while the shell is soft—green them
with salt and water as before directed; when a good
green, soak them in plain vinegar for a fortnight, and
put them in the yellow pickle pot.

## TO PICKLE ASPARAGUS.

POUR boiling salt and water on, and cover them
close—next day, take them out, dry them, and after
standing in vinegar, put them with the yellow pickle

## OBSERVATIONS ON PICKLING.

THE vessels for keeping pickles should be made of
stone ware, straight from the bottom to the top, with
stone covers to them; when the mouth is very wide,

the pickles may be taken out without breaking them The motive for keeping all pickles in plain vinegar, previous to putting them in the prepared pot, is to draw off the water with which they are saturated, that they may not weaken the vinegar of the pot. Pickles keep much better when the vinegar is not boiled.

---

# CORDIALS, &c.

---

### GINGER WINE.

To three gallons of water, put three pounds of sugar, and four ounces of race ginger, washed in many waters to cleanse it; boil them together for one hour, and strain it through a sieve; when lukewarm, put it in a cask with three lemons cut in slices, and two gills of beer yeast; shake it well, and stop the cask very tight; let it stand a week to ferment; and if not clear enough to bottle, it must remain until it becomes so; it will be fit to drink in ten days after bottling.

---

### ORGEAT,
#### *A Necessary Refreshment at all Parties.*

BOIL two quarts of milk with a stick of cinnamon and let it stand to be quite cold, first taking out the cinnamon; blanch four ounces of the best sweet almonds, pound them in a marble mortar with a little rose-water; mix them well with the milk, sweeten it to your taste, and let it boil a few minutes only, lest the almonds should be oily; strain it through a very fine sieve till quite smooth, and free from the almonds, serve it up either cold or lukewarm, in glasses with handles.

## CHERRY SHRUB.

GATHER ripe morello cherries, pick them from the stalk, and put them in an earthen pot, which must be set into an iron pot of water; make the water boil, but take care that none of it gets into the cherries; when the juice is extracted, pour it into a bag made of tolerably thick cloth, which will permit the juice to pass, but not the pulp of your cherries; sweeten it to your taste, and when it becomes perfectly clear, bottle it—put a gill of brandy into each bottle, before you pour in the juice—cover the corks with rosin. It will keep all summer, in a dry cool place, and is delicious mixed with water.

## CURRANT WINE.

GATHER full ripe currants on a dry day, pick them from the stalks, and weigh them; then crush them with your hands, leaving none whole; for every two pounds of currants put one quart of water; stir all well together, and let it stand three hours, and strain the liquor through a sieve; then, for every three pounds of currants, put one pound of powdered loaf sugar; stir it till the sugar is dissolved, boil it, and keep skimming it, as long as any scum will rise; let it stand sixteen hours to cool, before you put it in the cask—stop it very close. If the quantity be twenty gallons, let it stand three weeks before you bottle it; if it be thirty gallons, it must remain a month; it should be perfectly clear when drawn off—put a lump of sugar in each bottle, cork it well, and keep it in a cool place, or it will turn sour. This is a pleasant and cheap wine—and if properly made, will keep good for many years. It makes an agreeable beverage for the sick, when mixed with water.

## TO MAKE CHERRY BRANDY.

GET equal quantities of morello and common black cherries; fill your cask, and pour on (to a ten gallon cask) one gallon of boiling water; in two or three hours, fill it up with brandy—let it stand a week, then draw off all, and put another gallon of boiling water, and fill it again with brandy—at the end of the week, draw the whole off, empty the cask of the cherries, and pour in your brandy with water, to reduce the strength; first dissolving one pound of brown sugar in each gallon of your mixture. If the brandy be very strong, it will bear water enough to make the cask full.

## ROSE BRANDY.

GATHER leaves from fragrant roses without bruising, fill a pitcher with them, and cover them with French brandy; next day, pour off the brandy, take out the leaves, and fill the pitcher with fresh ones, and re-turn the brandy; do this till it is strongly impregnated, then bottle it; keep the pitcher closely covered during the process. It is better than distilled rose water for cakes, &c.

## PEACH CORDIAL.

GATHER ripe cling-stone peaches, wipe off the down, cut them to the stone in several places, and put them in a cask; when filled with peaches, pour on as much peach brandy as the cask will hold; let it stand six or eight weeks, then draw it off, put in water until re-duced to the strength of wine; to each gallon of this, add one pound of good brown sugar—dissolve it, and pour the cordial into a cask just large enough to hold it—when perfectly clear, it is fit for use.

## RASPBERRY CORDIAL.

To each quart of ripe red raspberries, put one quart of best French brandy; let it remain about a week, then strain it through a sieve or bag, pressing out all the liquid; when you have got as much as you want, reduce the strength to your taste with water, and put a pound of powdered loaf sugar to each gallon—let it stand till refined. Strawberry cordial is made the same way. It destroys the flavour of these fruits to put them on the fire.

## RASPBERRY VINEGAR.

Put a quart of ripe red raspberries in a bowl; pour on them a quart of strong well flavoured vinegar—let them stand twenty-four hours, strain them through a bag, put this liquid on another quart of fresh raspberries, which strain in the same manner—and then on a third quart: when this last is prepared, make it very sweet with pounded loaf sugar; refine and bottle it. It is a delicious beverage mixed with iced water.

## MINT CORDIAL.

Pick the mint early in the morning while the dew is on it, and be careful not to bruise it; pour some water over it, and drain it—put two handsful into a pitcher, with a quart of French brandy, cover it, and let it stand till next day; take the mint carefully out, and put in as much more, which must be taken out next day—do this the third time: then put three quarts of water to the brandy, and one pound of loaf sugar powdered; mix it well together—and when perfectly clear, bottle it.

---

## HYDROMEL, OR MEAD.

Mix your mead in the proportion of thirty-six ounces of honey to four quarts of warm water; when the honey is completely held in solution, pour it into a cask. When fermented, and become perfectly clear, bottle and cork it well. If properly prepared, it is a pleasant and wholesome drink; and in summer particularly grateful, on account of the large quantity of carbonic acid gas which it contains. Its goodness, however, depends greatly on the *time* of bottling, and other circumstances, which can only be acquired by practice.

---

## TO MAKE A SUBSTITUTE FOR ARRACK.

Dissolve two scruples flowers of Benzoin, in one quart of good rum.

---

## LEMON CORDIAL.

Cut six fresh lemons in thin slices, put them into a quart and a half of milk, boil it until the whey is very clear, then pass it through a sieve; put to this whey, one and a half quarts of French brandy, and three pounds of powdered loaf sugar; stir it till the sugar is dissolved—let it stand to refine, and bottle it; pare some of the yellow rind of the lemons very thin, and put a little in each bottle.

## GINGER BEER.

POUR two gallons of boiling water on two pounds brown sugar, one and a half ounce of cream of tartar, and the same of pounded ginger; stir them well, and put it in a small cask; when milk warm, put in half a pint of good yeast, shake the cask well, and stop it close—in twenty-four hours it will be fit to bottle—cork it very well, and in ten days it will sparkle like Champaigne—one or two lemons cut in slices and put in, will improve it much. For economy, you may use molasses instead of sugar—one quart in place of two pounds. This is a wholesome and delicious beverage in warm weather.

## SPRUCE BEER.

BOIL a handful of hops, and twice as much of the chippings of sassafras root, in ten gallons of water; strain it, and pour in, while hot, one gallon of molasses, two spoonsful of the essence of spruce, two spoonsful of powdered ginger, and one of pounded allspice; put it in a cask—when sufficiently cold, add half a pint of good yeast; stir it well, stop it close, and when fermented and clear, bottle and cork it tight.

## MOLASSES BEER.

PUT five quarts of hops, and five of wheat bran, into fifteen gallons of water; boil it three or four hours, strain it, and pour it into a cask with one head taken out; put in five quarts of molasses, stir it till well mixed, throw a cloth over the barrel; when moderately warm, add a quart of good yeast, which must be stirred in; then stop it close with a cloth and board. When it has fermented and become quite clear, bottle it—the corks should be soaked in boiling water an hour or two, and the bottles perfectly clean, and well drained.

## TO KEEP LEMON-JUICE.

GET lemons quite free from blemish, squeeze them, and strain the juice; to each pint of it, put a pound of good loaf sugar pounded; stir it frequently until the sugar is completely dissolved, cover the pitcher closely, and let it stand till the dregs have subsided, and the syrup is transparent; have bottles perfectly clean and dry, put a wine glass full of French brandy into each bottle, fill it with syrup, cork it, and dip the neck into melted rosin or pitch; keep them in a cool dry cellar— do not put it on the fire—it will destroy the fine flavour of the juice.

Pour water on the peels of the lemons, let them soak till you can scrape all the white pulp off, then boil the peel till soft; preserve them with half their weight of sugar, and keep them for mince pies, cakes, &c.  They are a very good substitute for citron.

## SUGAR VINEGAR.

To one measure of sugar, put seven measures of water moderately warm; dissolve it completely—put it into a cask, stir in yeast in the proportion of a pint to eight gallons: stop it close, and keep it in a warm place till sufficiently sour.

## HONEY VINEGAR.

To one quart of clear honey, put eight quarts of warm water; mix it well together: when it has passed through the acetous fermentation, a white vinegar will be formed, in many respects better than the ordinary vinegar.

## SYRUP OF VINEGAR.

Boil two pounds of sugar with four quarts of vine
gar, down to a syrup, and bottle it. This makes an
excellent beverage when mixed with water, either with
or without the addition of brandy. It is nearly equal
in flavour to the syrup of lime juice, when made with
superior vinegar.

## AROMATIC VINEGAR.

Put a portion of acetate of potash, (sal diureticus,)
into a smelling bottle; mix gradually with it half its
weight of sulphuric acid, and add a few drops of oil
of lavender.

## VINEGAR OF THE FOUR THIEVES.

Take lavender, rosemary, sage, wormwood, rue,
and mint, of each a large handful; put them in a pot
of earthen ware, pour on them four quarts of very
strong vinegar, cover the pot closely, and put a board
on the top; keep it in the hottest sun two weeks,
then strain and bottle it, putting in each bottle a clove
of garlic. When it has settled in the bottle and become clear, pour it off gently; do this until you get
it all free from sediment. The proper time to make
it is when the herbs are in full vigour, in June. This
vinegar is very refreshing in crowded rooms, in the
apartments of the sick; and is peculiarly grateful
when sprinkled about the house in damp weather.

## LAVENDER WATER.

Put a pint of highly rectified spirits of wine, to
one ounce of essential oil of lavender, and two

drachms of ambergris; shake them well together, and keep it closely stopped.

## HUNGARIAN WATER.

ONE pint spirits of wine, one ounce oil of rosemary, and two drachms essence of ambergris.

## TO PREPARE COSMETIC SOAP FOR WASH-ING THE HANDS.

TAKE a pound of castile, or any other nice old soap; scrape it in small pieces, and put it on the fire with a little water—stir it till it becomes a smooth paste, pour it into a bowl, and when cold, add some lavender water, or essence of any kind—beat it with a silver spoon until well mixed, thicken it with corn meal, and keep it in small pots closely covered—for the admission of air will soon make the soap hard.

## COLOGNE WATER.

THREE quarts spirits of wine, six drachms oil of lavender, one drachm oil of rosemary, three drachms essence of lemon, ten drops oil of cinnamon—mix them together very well.

## SOFT POMATUM.

GET nice sweet lard that has no salt in it—put in any agreeable perfume, beat it to a cream, and put it in small pots.

## TO MAKE SOAP.

PUT on the fire any quantity of lye you choose that is strong enough to bear an egg—to each gallon, add three quarters of a pound of clean grease: boil it very fast, and stir it frequently—a few hours will suffice to make it good soap. When you find by cooling a little on a plate that it is a thick jelly, and no grease appears, put in salt in the proportion of one pint to three gallons—let it boil a few minutes, and pour it in tubs to cool—(should the soap be thin, add a little water to that in the plate, stir it well, and by that means ascertain how much water is necessary for the whole quantity; very strong lye will require water to thicken it, after the incorporation is complete; this must be done before the salt is added.) Next day, cut out the soap, melt it, and cool it again; this takes out all the lye, and keeps the soap from shrinking when dried. A strict conformity to these rules, will banish the lunar bugbear, which has so long annoyed soap makers. Should cracknels be used, there must be one pound to each gallon. Kitchen grease should be clarified in a quantity of water, or the salt will prevent its incorporating with the lye. Soft soap is made in the same manner, only omitting the salt. It may also be made by putting the lye and grease together in exact proportions, and placing it under the influence of a hot sun for eight or ten days, stirring it well four or five times a day.

## TO MAKE STARCH.

Wash a peck of good wheat, and pick it very clean; put it in a tub, and cover it with water; it must be kept in the sun, and the water changed every day, or it will smell very offensively. When the wheat becomes quite soft, it must be well rubbed in the hands, and the husks thrown into another tub; let this white substance settle, then pour off the water, put on fresh, stir it up well, and let it subside; do this every day till the water comes off clear—then pour it off; collect the starch in a bag, tie it up tight, and set it in the sun a few days: then open it, and dry the starch on dishes.

## TO DRY HERBS.

GATHER them on a dry day, just before they begin to blossom; brush off the dust, cut them in small branches, and dry them quickly in a moderate oven; pick off the leaves when dry, pound and sift them—bottle them immediately, and cork them closely. They must be kept in a dry place.

## TO CLEAN SILVER UTENSILS.

DISSOLVE two tea-spoonsful of alum in a quart of moderately strong lye—stir in a gill of soft soap, and skim off the dross. Wash the silver clean in hot water, let it remain covered with this mixture for ten or fifteen minutes, turning it over frequently; then wash it in hot soap suds, and rub it well with a dry cloth.

## TO MAKE BLACKING.

A QUARTER of a pound of ivory black, two ounces of sugar candy, a quarter of an ounce of gum tragacanth; pound them all very fine, boil a bottle of porter, and stir the ingredients in while boiling hot.

## TO CLEAN KNIVES AND FORKS.

WASH them in warm water, and wipe them till quite dry; then touch them lightly over, without smearing the handles, with rotten stone made wet; let it dry on them, and then rub with a clean cloth until they are bright. With this mode of cleaning, one set of knives and forks will serve a family twenty years; they will require the frequent use of a steel to keep them with a keen edge—but must never be put into very hot water, lest the handles be injured

### THE END.

A CATALOG OF SELECTED
# DOVER BOOKS
## IN SCIENCE AND MATHEMATICS

# Astronomy

BURNHAM'S CELESTIAL HANDBOOK, Robert Burnham, Jr. Thorough guide to the stars beyond our solar system. Exhaustive treatment. Alphabetical by constellation: Andromeda to Cetus in Vol. 1; Chamaeleon to Orion in Vol. 2; and Pavo to Vulpecula in Vol. 3. Hundreds of illustrations. Index in Vol. 3. 2,000pp. 6⅛ x 9¼.

Vol. I: 0-486-23567-X
Vol. II: 0-486-23568-8
Vol. III: 0-486-23673-0

EXPLORING THE MOON THROUGH BINOCULARS AND SMALL TELE-SCOPES, Ernest H. Cherrington, Jr. Informative, profusely illustrated guide to locating and identifying craters, rills, seas, mountains, other lunar features. Newly revised and updated with special section of new photos. Over 100 photos and diagrams. 240pp. 8¼ x 11. 0-486-24491-1

THE EXTRATERRESTRIAL LIFE DEBATE, 1750–1900, Michael J. Crowe. First detailed, scholarly study in English of the many ideas that developed from 1750 to 1900 regarding the existence of intelligent extraterrestrial life. Examines ideas of Kant, Herschel, Voltaire, Percival Lowell, many other scientists and thinkers. 16 illustrations. 704pp. 5⅜ x 8½. 0-486-40675-X

THEORIES OF THE WORLD FROM ANTIQUITY TO THE COPERNICAN REVOLUTION, Michael J. Crowe. Newly revised edition of an accessible, enlightening book re-creates the change from an earth-centered to a sun-centered conception of the solar system. 242pp. 5⅜ x 8½. 0-486-41444-2

ARISTARCHUS OF SAMOS: The Ancient Copernicus, Sir Thomas Heath. Heath's history of astronomy ranges from Homer and Hesiod to Aristarchus and includes quotes from numerous thinkers, compilers, and scholasticists from Thales and Anaximander through Pythagoras, Plato, Aristotle, and Heraclides. 34 figures. 448pp. 5⅜ x 8½.
0-486-43886-4

A COMPLETE MANUAL OF AMATEUR ASTRONOMY: TOOLS AND TECHNIQUES FOR ASTRONOMICAL OBSERVATIONS, P. Clay Sherrod with Thomas L. Koed. Concise, highly readable book discusses: selecting, setting up and maintaining a telescope; amateur studies of the sun; lunar topography and occultations; observations of Mars, Jupiter, Saturn, the minor planets and the stars; an introduction to photoelectric photometry; more. 1981 ed. 124 figures. 25 halftones. 37 tables. 335pp. 6½ x 9¼. 0-486-42820-8

AMATEUR ASTRONOMER'S HANDBOOK, J. B. Sidgwick. Timeless, comprehensive coverage of telescopes, mirrors, lenses, mountings, telescope drives, micrometers, spectroscopes, more. 189 illustrations. 576pp. 5⅝ x 8¼. (Available in U.S. only.)
0-486-24034-7

STAR LORE: Myths, Legends, and Facts, William Tyler Olcott. Captivating retellings of the origins and histories of ancient star groups include Pegasus, Ursa Major, Pleiades, signs of the zodiac, and other constellations. "Classic."—Sky & Telescope. 58 illustrations. 544pp. 5⅜ x 8½. 0-486-43581-4

# Chemistry

THE SCEPTICAL CHYMIST: THE CLASSIC 1661 TEXT, Robert Boyle. Boyle defines the term "element," asserting that all natural phenomena can be explained by the motion and organization of primary particles. 1911 ed. viii+232pp. $5^3/8$ x $8^1/2$.
0-486-42825-7

RADIOACTIVE SUBSTANCES, Marie Curie. Here is the celebrated scientist's doctoral thesis, the prelude to her receipt of the 1903 Nobel Prize. Curie discusses establishing atomic character of radioactivity found in compounds of uranium and thorium; extraction from pitchblende of polonium and radium; isolation of pure radium chloride; determination of atomic weight of radium; plus electric, photographic, luminous, heat, color effects of radioactivity. ii+94pp. $5^3/8$ x $8^1/2$.
0-486-42550-9

CHEMICAL MAGIC, Leonard A. Ford. Second Edition, Revised by E. Winston Grundmeier. Over 100 unusual stunts demonstrating cold fire, dust explosions, much more. Text explains scientific principles and stresses safety precautions. 128pp. $5^3/8$ x $8^1/2$.
0-486-67628-5

MOLECULAR THEORY OF CAPILLARITY, J. S. Rowlinson and B. Widom. History of surface phenomena offers critical and detailed examination and assessment of modern theories, focusing on statistical mechanics and application of results in mean-field approximation to model systems. 1989 edition. 352pp. $5^3/8$ x $8^1/2$.
0-486-42544-4

CHEMICAL AND CATALYTIC REACTION ENGINEERING, James J. Carberry. Designed to offer background for managing chemical reactions, this text examines behavior of chemical reactions and reactors; fluid-fluid and fluid-solid reaction systems; heterogeneous catalysis and catalytic kinetics; more. 1976 edition. 672pp. $6^1/8$ x $9^1/4$.
0-486-41736-0 $31.95

ELEMENTS OF CHEMISTRY, Antoine Lavoisier. Monumental classic by founder of modern chemistry in remarkable reprint of rare 1790 Kerr translation. A must for every student of chemistry or the history of science. 539pp. $5^3/8$ x $8^1/2$.
0-486-64624-6

MOLECULES AND RADIATION: An Introduction to Modern Molecular Spectroscopy. Second Edition, Jeffrey I. Steinfeld. This unified treatment introduces upper-level undergraduates and graduate students to the concepts and the methods of molecular spectroscopy and applications to quantum electronics, lasers, and related optical phenomena. 1985 edition. 512pp. $5^3/8$ x $8^1/2$.
0-486-44152-0

A SHORT HISTORY OF CHEMISTRY, J. R. Partington. Classic exposition explores origins of chemistry, alchemy, early medical chemistry, nature of atmosphere, theory of valency, laws and structure of atomic theory, much more. 428pp. $5^3/8$ x $8^1/2$. (Available in U.S. only.)
0-486-65977-1

GENERAL CHEMISTRY, Linus Pauling. Revised 3rd edition of classic first-year text by Nobel laureate. Atomic and molecular structure, quantum mechanics, statistical mechanics, thermodynamics correlated with descriptive chemistry. Problems. 992pp. $5^3/8$ x $8^1/2$.
0-486-65622-5

ELECTRON CORRELATION IN MOLECULES, S. Wilson. This text addresses one of theoretical chemistry's central problems. Topics include molecular electronic structure, independent electron models, electron correlation, the linked diagram theorem, and related topics. 1984 edition. 304pp. $5^3/8$ x $8^1/2$.
0-486-45879-2

# Engineering

DE RE METALLICA, Georgius Agricola. The famous Hoover translation of greatest treatise on technological chemistry, engineering, geology, mining of early modern times (1556). All 289 original woodcuts. 638pp. 6¾ x 11.　　　　　　　　0-486-60006-8

FUNDAMENTALS OF ASTRODYNAMICS, Roger Bate et al. Modern approach developed by U.S. Air Force Academy. Designed as a first course. Problems, exercises. Numerous illustrations. 455pp. 5⅜ x 8½.　　　　　　　　0-486-60061-0

DYNAMICS OF FLUIDS IN POROUS MEDIA, Jacob Bear. For advanced students of ground water hydrology, soil mechanics and physics, drainage and irrigation engineering and more. 335 illustrations. Exercises, with answers. 784pp. 6⅛ x 9¼.　　0-486-65675-6

THEORY OF VISCOELASTICITY (SECOND EDITION), Richard M. Christensen. Complete consistent description of the linear theory of the viscoelastic behavior of materials. Problem-solving techniques discussed. 1982 edition. 29 figures. xiv+364pp. 6⅛ x 9¼.
　　　　　　　　0-486-42880-X

MECHANICS, J. P. Den Hartog. A classic introductory text or refresher. Hundreds of applications and design problems illuminate fundamentals of trusses, loaded beams and cables, etc. 334 answered problems. 462pp. 5⅜ x 8½.　　　　　　0-486-60754-2

MECHANICAL VIBRATIONS, J. P. Den Hartog. Classic textbook offers lucid explanations and illustrative models, applying theories of vibrations to a variety of practical industrial engineering problems. Numerous figures. 233 problems, solutions. Appendix. Index. Preface. 436pp. 5⅜ x 8½.　　　　　　　　0-486-64785-4

STRENGTH OF MATERIALS, J. P. Den Hartog. Full, clear treatment of basic material (tension, torsion, bending, etc.) plus advanced material on engineering methods, applications. 350 answered problems. 323pp. 5⅜ x 8½.　　　　0-486-60755-0

A HISTORY OF MECHANICS, René Dugas. Monumental study of mechanical principles from antiquity to quantum mechanics. Contributions of ancient Greeks, Galileo, Leonardo, Kepler, Lagrange, many others. 671pp. 5⅜ x 8½.　　　0-486-65632-2

STABILITY THEORY AND ITS APPLICATIONS TO STRUCTURAL MECHANICS, Clive L. Dym. Self-contained text focuses on Koiter postbuckling analyses, with mathematical notions of stability of motion. Basing minimum energy principles for static stability upon dynamic concepts of stability of motion, it develops asymptotic buckling and postbuckling analyses from potential energy considerations, with applications to columns, plates, and arches. 1974 ed. 208pp. 5⅜ x 8½.　　　0-486-42541-X

BASIC ELECTRICITY, U.S. Bureau of Naval Personnel. Originally a training course; best nontechnical coverage. Topics include batteries, circuits, conductors, AC and DC, inductance and capacitance, generators, motors, transformers, amplifiers, etc. Many questions with answers. 349 illustrations. 1969 edition. 448pp. 6½ x 9¼.　　0-486-20973-3

ROCKETS, Robert Goddard. Two of the most significant publications in the history of rocketry and jet propulsion: "A Method of Reaching Extreme Altitudes" (1919) and "Liquid Propellant Rocket Development" (1936). 128pp. 5⅜ x 8½. 0-486-42537-1

STATISTICAL MECHANICS: PRINCIPLES AND APPLICATIONS, Terrell L. Hill. Standard text covers fundamentals of statistical mechanics, applications to fluctuation theory, imperfect gases, distribution functions, more. 448pp. 5⅜ x 8½. 0-486-65390-0

ENGINEERING AND TECHNOLOGY 1650–1750: ILLUSTRATIONS AND TEXTS FROM ORIGINAL SOURCES, Martin Jensen. Highly readable text with more than 200 contemporary drawings and detailed engravings of engineering projects dealing with surveying, leveling, materials, hand tools, lifting equipment, transport and erection, piling, bailing, water supply, hydraulic engineering, and more. Among the specific projects outlined-transporting a 50-ton stone to the Louvre, erecting an obelisk, building timber locks, and dredging canals. 207pp. 8⅜ x 11¼. 0-486-42232-1

THE VARIATIONAL PRINCIPLES OF MECHANICS, Cornelius Lanczos. Graduate level coverage of calculus of variations, equations of motion, relativistic mechanics, more. First inexpensive paperbound edition of classic treatise. Index. Bibliography. 418pp. 5⅜ x 8½. 0-486-65067-7

PROTECTION OF ELECTRONIC CIRCUITS FROM OVERVOLTAGES, Ronald B. Standler. Five-part treatment presents practical rules and strategies for circuits designed to protect electronic systems from damage by transient overvoltages. 1989 ed. xxiv+434pp. 6⅛ x 9¼. 0-486-42552-5

ROTARY WING AERODYNAMICS, W. Z. Stepniewski. Clear, concise text covers aerodynamic phenomena of the rotor and offers guidelines for helicopter performance evaluation. Originally prepared for NASA. 537 figures. 640pp. 6⅛ x 9¼. 0-486-64647-5

INTRODUCTION TO SPACE DYNAMICS, William Tyrrell Thomson. Comprehensive, classic introduction to space-flight engineering for advanced undergraduate and graduate students. Includes vector algebra, kinematics, transformation of coordinates. Bibliography. Index. 352pp. 5⅜ x 8½. 0-486-65113-4

HISTORY OF STRENGTH OF MATERIALS, Stephen P. Timoshenko. Excellent historical survey of the strength of materials with many references to the theories of elasticity and structure. 245 figures. 452pp. 5⅜ x 8½. 0-486-61187-6

ANALYTICAL FRACTURE MECHANICS, David J. Unger. Self-contained text supplements standard fracture mechanics texts by focusing on analytical methods for determining crack-tip stress and strain fields. 336pp. 6⅛ x 9¼. 0-486-41737-9

STATISTICAL MECHANICS OF ELASTICITY, J. H. Weiner. Advanced, self-contained treatment illustrates general principles and elastic behavior of solids. Part 1, based on classical mechanics, studies thermoelastic behavior of crystalline and polymeric solids. Part 2, based on quantum mechanics, focuses on interatomic force laws, behavior of solids, and thermally activated processes. For students of physics and chemistry and for polymer physicists. 1983 ed. 96 figures. 496pp. 5⅜ x 8½. 0-486-42260-7

# Mathematics

FUNCTIONAL ANALYSIS (Second Corrected Edition), George Bachman and Lawrence Narici. Excellent treatment of subject geared toward students with background in linear algebra, advanced calculus, physics and engineering. Text covers introduction to inner-product spaces, normed, metric spaces, and topological spaces; complete orthonormal sets, the Hahn-Banach Theorem and its consequences, and many other related subjects. 1966 ed. 544pp. 6⅛ x 9¼. 0-486-40251-7

DIFFERENTIAL MANIFOLDS, Antoni A. Kosinski. Introductory text for advanced undergraduates and graduate students presents systematic study of the topological structure of smooth manifolds, starting with elements of theory and concluding with method of surgery. 1993 edition. 288pp. 5⅜ x 8½. 0-486-46244-7

VECTOR AND TENSOR ANALYSIS WITH APPLICATIONS, A. I. Borisenko and I. E. Tarapov. Concise introduction. Worked-out problems, solutions, exercises. 257pp. 5⅝ x 8¼. 0-486-63833-2

AN INTRODUCTION TO ORDINARY DIFFERENTIAL EQUATIONS, Earl A. Coddington. A thorough and systematic first course in elementary differential equations for undergraduates in mathematics and science, with many exercises and problems (with answers). Index. 304pp. 5⅜ x 8½. 0-486-65942-9

FOURIER SERIES AND ORTHOGONAL FUNCTIONS, Harry F. Davis. An incisive text combining theory and practical example to introduce Fourier series, orthogonal functions and applications of the Fourier method to boundary-value problems. 570 exercises. Answers and notes. 416pp. 5⅜ x 8½. 0-486-65973-9

COMPUTABILITY AND UNSOLVABILITY, Martin Davis. Classic graduate-level introduction to theory of computability, usually referred to as theory of recurrent functions. New preface and appendix. 288pp. 5⅜ x 8½. 0-486-61471-9

AN INTRODUCTION TO MATHEMATICAL ANALYSIS, Robert A. Rankin. Dealing chiefly with functions of a single real variable, this text by a distinguished educator introduces limits, continuity, differentiability, integration, convergence of infinite series, double series, and infinite products. 1963 edition. 624pp. 5⅜ x 8½. 0-486-46251-X

METHODS OF NUMERICAL INTEGRATION (SECOND EDITION), Philip J. Davis and Philip Rabinowitz. Requiring only a background in calculus, this text covers approximate integration over finite and infinite intervals, error analysis, approximate integration in two or more dimensions, and automatic integration. 1984 edition. 624pp. 5⅜ x 8½. 0-486-45339-1

INTRODUCTION TO LINEAR ALGEBRA AND DIFFERENTIAL EQUATIONS, John W. Dettman. Excellent text covers complex numbers, determinants, orthonormal bases, Laplace transforms, much more. Exercises with solutions. Undergraduate level. 416pp. 5⅜ x 8½. 0-486-65191-6

RIEMANN'S ZETA FUNCTION, H. M. Edwards. Superb, high-level study of landmark 1859 publication entitled "On the Number of Primes Less Than a Given Magnitude" traces developments in mathematical theory that it inspired. xiv+315pp. 5⅜ x 8½. 0-486-41740-9

CALCULUS OF VARIATIONS WITH APPLICATIONS, George M. Ewing. Applications-oriented introduction to variational theory develops insight and promotes understanding of specialized books, research papers. Suitable for advanced undergraduate/graduate students as primary, supplementary text. 352pp. 5³/₈ x 8¹/₂.
0-486-64856-7

MATHEMATICIAN'S DELIGHT, W. W. Sawyer. "Recommended with confidence" by *The Times Literary Supplement*, this lively survey was written by a renowned teacher. It starts with arithmetic and algebra, gradually proceeding to trigonometry and calculus. 1943 edition. 240pp. 5³/₈ x 8¹/₂.
0-486-46240-4

ADVANCED EUCLIDEAN GEOMETRY, Roger A. Johnson. This classic text explores the geometry of the triangle and the circle, concentrating on extensions of Euclidean theory, and examining in detail many relatively recent theorems. 1929 edition. 336pp. 5³/₈ x 8¹/₂.
0-486-46237-4

COUNTEREXAMPLES IN ANALYSIS, Bernard R. Gelbaum and John M. H. Olmsted. These counterexamples deal mostly with the part of analysis known as "real variables." The first half covers the real number system, and the second half encompasses higher dimensions. 1962 edition. xxiv+198pp. 5³/₈ x 8¹/₂.
0-486-42875-3

CATASTROPHE THEORY FOR SCIENTISTS AND ENGINEERS, Robert Gilmore. Advanced-level treatment describes mathematics of theory grounded in the work of Poincaré, R. Thom, other mathematicians. Also important applications to problems in mathematics, physics, chemistry and engineering. 1981 edition. References. 28 tables. 397 black-and-white illustrations. xvii + 666pp. 6¹/₈ x 9¹/₄.
0-486-67539-4

COMPLEX VARIABLES: Second Edition, Robert B. Ash and W. P. Novinger. Suitable for advanced undergraduates and graduate students, this newly revised treatment covers Cauchy theorem and its applications, analytic functions, and the prime number theorem. Numerous problems and solutions. 2004 edition. 224pp. 6¹/₂ x 9¹/₄.
0-486-46250-1

NUMERICAL METHODS FOR SCIENTISTS AND ENGINEERS, Richard Hamming. Classic text stresses frequency approach in coverage of algorithms, polynomial approximation, Fourier approximation, exponential approximation, other topics. Revised and enlarged 2nd edition. 721pp. 5³/₈ x 8¹/₂.
0-486-65241-6

INTRODUCTION TO NUMERICAL ANALYSIS (2nd Edition), F. B. Hildebrand. Classic, fundamental treatment covers computation, approximation, interpolation, numerical differentiation and integration, other topics. 150 new problems. 669pp. 5³/₈ x 8¹/₂.
0-486-65363-3

MARKOV PROCESSES AND POTENTIAL THEORY, Robert M. Blumental and Ronald K. Getoor. This graduate-level text explores the relationship between Markov processes and potential theory in terms of excessive functions, multiplicative functionals and subprocesses, additive functionals and their potentials, and dual processes. 1968 edition. 320pp. 5³/₈ x 8¹/₂.
0-486-46263-3

ABSTRACT SETS AND FINITE ORDINALS: An Introduction to the Study of Set Theory, G. B. Keene. This text unites logical and philosophical aspects of set theory in a manner intelligible to mathematicians without training in formal logic and to logicians without a mathematical background. 1961 edition. 112pp. 5³/₈ x 8¹/₂.
0-486-46249-8

INTRODUCTORY REAL ANALYSIS, A.N. Kolmogorov, S. V. Fomin. Translated by Richard A. Silverman. Self-contained, evenly paced introduction to real and functional analysis. Some 350 problems. 403pp. 5⅜ x 8½.                    0-486-61226-0

APPLIED ANALYSIS, Cornelius Lanczos. Classic work on analysis and design of finite processes for approximating solution of analytical problems. Algebraic equations, matrices, harmonic analysis, quadrature methods, much more. 559pp. 5⅜ x 8½.   0-486-65656-X

AN INTRODUCTION TO ALGEBRAIC STRUCTURES, Joseph Landin. Superb self-contained text covers "abstract algebra": sets and numbers, theory of groups, theory of rings, much more. Numerous well-chosen examples, exercises. 247pp. 5⅜ x 8½.
0-486-65940-2

QUALITATIVE THEORY OF DIFFERENTIAL EQUATIONS, V. V. Nemytskii and V.V. Stepanov. Classic graduate-level text by two prominent Soviet mathematicians covers classical differential equations as well as topological dynamics and ergodic theory. Bibliographies. 523pp. 5⅜ x 8½.                    0-486-65954-2

THEORY OF MATRICES, Sam Perlis. Outstanding text covering rank, nonsingularity and inverses in connection with the development of canonical matrices under the relation of equivalence, and without the intervention of determinants. Includes exercises. 237pp. 5⅜ x 8½.                    0-486-66810-X

INTRODUCTION TO ANALYSIS, Maxwell Rosenlicht. Unusually clear, accessible coverage of set theory, real number system, metric spaces, continuous functions, Riemann integration, multiple integrals, more. Wide range of problems. Undergraduate level. Bibliography. 254pp. 5⅜ x 8½.                    0-486-65038-3

MODERN NONLINEAR EQUATIONS, Thomas L. Saaty. Emphasizes practical solution of problems; covers seven types of equations. ". . . a welcome contribution to the existing literature. . . ."—*Math Reviews.* 490pp. 5⅜ x 8½.          0-486-64232-1

MATRICES AND LINEAR ALGEBRA, Hans Schneider and George Phillip Barker. Basic textbook covers theory of matrices and its applications to systems of linear equations and related topics such as determinants, eigenvalues and differential equations. Numerous exercises. 432pp. 5⅜ x 8½.                    0-486-66014-1

LINEAR ALGEBRA, Georgi E. Shilov. Determinants, linear spaces, matrix algebras, similar topics. For advanced undergraduates, graduates. Silverman translation. 387pp. 5⅜ x 8½.                    0-486-63518-X

MATHEMATICAL METHODS OF GAME AND ECONOMIC THEORY: Revised Edition, Jean-Pierre Aubin. This text begins with optimization theory and convex analysis, followed by topics in game theory and mathematical economics, and concluding with an introduction to nonlinear analysis and control theory. 1982 edition. 656pp. 6⅛ x 9¼.
0-486-46265-X

SET THEORY AND LOGIC, Robert R. Stoll. Lucid introduction to unified theory of mathematical concepts. Set theory and logic seen as tools for conceptual understanding of real number system. 496pp. 5⅜ x 8¼.                    0-486-63829-4

TENSOR CALCULUS, J.L. Synge and A. Schild. Widely used introductory text covers spaces and tensors, basic operations in Riemannian space, non-Riemannian spaces, etc. 324pp. $5^{3}/_{8}$ x $8^{1}/_{4}$. 0-486-63612-7

ORDINARY DIFFERENTIAL EQUATIONS, Morris Tenenbaum and Harry Pollard. Exhaustive survey of ordinary differential equations for undergraduates in mathematics, engineering, science. Thorough analysis of theorems. Diagrams. Bibliography. Index. 818pp. $5^{3}/_{8}$ x $8^{1}/_{2}$. 0-486-64940-7

INTEGRAL EQUATIONS, F. G. Tricomi. Authoritative, well-written treatment of extremely useful mathematical tool with wide applications. Volterra Equations, Fredholm Equations, much more. Advanced undergraduate to graduate level. Exercises. Bibliography. 238pp. $5^{3}/_{8}$ x $8^{1}/_{2}$. 0-486-64828-1

FOURIER SERIES, Georgi P. Tolstov. Translated by Richard A. Silverman. A valuable addition to the literature on the subject, moving clearly from subject to subject and theorem to theorem. 107 problems, answers. 336pp. $5^{3}/_{8}$ x $8^{1}/_{2}$. 0-486-63317-9

INTRODUCTION TO MATHEMATICAL THINKING, Friedrich Waismann. Examinations of arithmetic, geometry, and theory of integers; rational and natural numbers; complete induction; limit and point of accumulation; remarkable curves; complex and hypercomplex numbers, more. 1959 ed. 27 figures. xii+260pp. $5^{3}/_{8}$ x $8^{1}/_{2}$. 0-486-42804-8

THE RADON TRANSFORM AND SOME OF ITS APPLICATIONS, Stanley R. Deans. Of value to mathematicians, physicists, and engineers, this excellent introduction covers both theory and applications, including a rich array of examples and literature. Revised and updated by the author. 1993 edition. 304pp. $6^{1}/_{8}$ x $9^{1}/_{4}$. 0-486-46241-2

CALCULUS OF VARIATIONS, Robert Weinstock. Basic introduction covering isoperimetric problems, theory of elasticity, quantum mechanics, electrostatics, etc. Exercises throughout. 326pp. $5^{3}/_{8}$ x $8^{1}/_{2}$. 0-486-63069-2

THE CONTINUUM: A CRITICAL EXAMINATION OF THE FOUNDATION OF ANALYSIS, Hermann Weyl. Classic of 20th-century foundational research deals with the conceptual problem posed by the continuum. 156pp. $5^{3}/_{8}$ x $8^{1}/_{2}$. 0-486-67982-9

CHALLENGING MATHEMATICAL PROBLEMS WITH ELEMENTARY SOLUTIONS, A. M. Yaglom and I. M. Yaglom. Over 170 challenging problems on probability theory, combinatorial analysis, points and lines, topology, convex polygons, many other topics. Solutions. Total of 445pp. $5^{3}/_{8}$ x $8^{1}/_{2}$. Two-vol. set.
Vol. I: 0-486-65536-9 Vol. II: 0-486-65537-7

INTRODUCTION TO PARTIAL DIFFERENTIAL EQUATIONS WITH APPLICATIONS, E. C. Zachmanoglou and Dale W. Thoe. Essentials of partial differential equations applied to common problems in engineering and the physical sciences. Problems and answers. 416pp. $5^{3}/_{8}$ x $8^{1}/_{2}$. 0-486-65251-3

STOCHASTIC PROCESSES AND FILTERING THEORY, Andrew H. Jazwinski. This unified treatment presents material previously available only in journals, and in terms accessible to engineering students. Although theory is emphasized, it discusses numerous practical applications as well. 1970 edition. 400pp. $5^{3}/_{8}$ x $8^{1}/_{2}$. 0-486-46274-9

# Math—Decision Theory, Statistics, Probability

INTRODUCTION TO PROBABILITY, John E. Freund. Featured topics include permutations and factorials, probabilities and odds, frequency interpretation, mathematical expectation, decision-making, postulates of probability, rule of elimination, much more. Exercises with some solutions. Summary. 1973 edition. 247pp. 5³/₈ x 8¹/₂.
0-486-67549-1

STATISTICAL AND INDUCTIVE PROBABILITIES, Hugues Leblanc. This treatment addresses a decades-old dispute among probability theorists, asserting that both statistical and inductive probabilities may be treated as sentence-theoretic measurements, and that the latter qualify as estimates of the former. 1962 edition. 160pp. 5³/₈ x 8¹/₂.
0-486-44980-7

APPLIED MULTIVARIATE ANALYSIS: Using Bayesian and Frequentist Methods of Inference, Second Edition, S. James Press. This two-part treatment deals with foundations as well as models and applications. Topics include continuous multivariate distributions; regression and analysis of variance; factor analysis and latent structure analysis; and structuring multivariate populations. 1982 edition. 692pp. 5³/₈ x 8¹/₂.      0-486-44236-5

LINEAR PROGRAMMING AND ECONOMIC ANALYSIS, Robert Dorfman, Paul A. Samuelson and Robert M. Solow. First comprehensive treatment of linear programming in standard economic analysis. Game theory, modern welfare economics, Leontief input-output, more. 525pp. 5³/₈ x 8¹/₂.      0-486-65491-5

PROBABILITY: AN INTRODUCTION, Samuel Goldberg. Excellent basic text covers set theory, probability theory for finite sample spaces, binomial theorem, much more. 360 problems. Bibliographies. 322pp. 5³/₈ x 8¹/₂.      0-486-65252-1

GAMES AND DECISIONS: INTRODUCTION AND CRITICAL SURVEY, R. Duncan Luce and Howard Raiffa. Superb nontechnical introduction to game theory, primarily applied to social sciences. Utility theory, zero-sum games, n-person games, decision-making, much more. Bibliography. 509pp. 5³/₈ x 8¹/₂.      0-486-65943-7

INTRODUCTION TO THE THEORY OF GAMES, J. C. C. McKinsey. This comprehensive overview of the mathematical theory of games illustrates applications to situations involving conflicts of interest, including economic, social, political, and military contexts. Appropriate for advanced undergraduate and graduate courses; advanced calculus a prerequisite. 1952 ed. x+372pp. 5³/₈ x 8¹/₂.      0-486-42811-7

FIFTY CHALLENGING PROBLEMS IN PROBABILITY WITH SOLUTIONS, Frederick Mosteller. Remarkable puzzlers, graded in difficulty, illustrate elementary and advanced aspects of probability. Detailed solutions. 88pp. 5³/₈ x 8¹/₂.      0-486-65355-2

PROBABILITY THEORY: A CONCISE COURSE, Y. A. Rozanov. Highly readable, self-contained introduction covers combination of events, dependent events, Bernoulli trials, etc. 148pp. 5³/₈ x 8¹/₄.      0-486-63544-9

THE STATISTICAL ANALYSIS OF EXPERIMENTAL DATA, John Mandel. First half of book presents fundamental mathematical definitions, concepts and facts while remaining half deals with statistics primarily as an interpretive tool. Well-written text, numerous worked examples with step-by-step presentation. Includes 116 tables. 448pp. 5³/₈ x 8¹/₂.      0-486-64666-1

# Math—Geometry and Topology

ELEMENTARY CONCEPTS OF TOPOLOGY, Paul Alexandroff. Elegant, intuitive approach to topology from set-theoretic topology to Betti groups; how concepts of topology are useful in math and physics. 25 figures. 57pp. 5⅜ x 8½.     0-486-60747-X

A LONG WAY FROM EUCLID, Constance Reid. Lively guide by a prominent historian focuses on the role of Euclid's Elements in subsequent mathematical developments. Elementary algebra and plane geometry are sole prerequisites. 80 drawings. 1963 edition. 304pp. 5⅜ x 8½.     0-486-43613-6

EXPERIMENTS IN TOPOLOGY, Stephen Barr. Classic, lively explanation of one of the byways of mathematics. Klein bottles, Moebius strips, projective planes, map coloring, problem of the Koenigsberg bridges, much more, described with clarity and wit. 43 figures. 210pp. 5⅜ x 8½.     0-486-25933-1

THE GEOMETRY OF RENÉ DESCARTES, René Descartes. The great work founded analytical geometry. Original French text, Descartes's own diagrams, together with definitive Smith-Latham translation. 244pp. 5⅜ x 8½.     0-486-60068-8

EUCLIDEAN GEOMETRY AND TRANSFORMATIONS, Clayton W. Dodge. This introduction to Euclidean geometry emphasizes transformations, particularly isometries and similarities. Suitable for undergraduate courses, it includes numerous examples, many with detailed answers. 1972 ed. viii+296pp. 6⅛ x 9¼.     0-486-43476-1

EXCURSIONS IN GEOMETRY, C. Stanley Ogilvy. A straightedge, compass, and a little thought are all that's needed to discover the intellectual excitement of geometry. Harmonic division and Apollonian circles, inversive geometry, hexlet, Golden Section, more. 132 illustrations. 192pp. 5⅜ x 8½.     0-486-26530-7

THE THIRTEEN BOOKS OF EUCLID'S ELEMENTS, translated with introduction and commentary by Sir Thomas L. Heath. Definitive edition. Textual and linguistic notes, mathematical analysis. 2,500 years of critical commentary. Unabridged. 1,414pp. 5⅜ x 8½. Three-vol. set.

    Vol. I: 0-486-60088-2    Vol. II: 0-486-60089-0    Vol. III: 0-486-60090-4

SPACE AND GEOMETRY: IN THE LIGHT OF PHYSIOLOGICAL, PSYCHOLOGICAL AND PHYSICAL INQUIRY, Ernst Mach. Three essays by an eminent philosopher and scientist explore the nature, origin, and development of our concepts of space, with a distinctness and precision suitable for undergraduate students and other readers. 1906 ed. vi+148pp. 5⅜ x 8½.     0-486-43909-7

GEOMETRY OF COMPLEX NUMBERS, Hans Schwerdtfeger. Illuminating, widely praised book on analytic geometry of circles, the Moebius transformation, and two-dimensional non-Euclidean geometries. 200pp. 5⅜ x 8¼.     0-486-63830-8

DIFFERENTIAL GEOMETRY, Heinrich W. Guggenheimer. Local differential geometry as an application of advanced calculus and linear algebra. Curvature, transformation groups, surfaces, more. Exercises. 62 figures. 378pp. 5⅜ x 8½.     0-486-63433-7

# History of Math

THE WORKS OF ARCHIMEDES, Archimedes (T. L. Heath, ed.). Topics include the famous problems of the ratio of the areas of a cylinder and an inscribed sphere; the measurement of a circle; the properties of conoids, spheroids, and spirals; and the quadrature of the parabola. Informative introduction. clxxxvi+326pp. $5\frac{3}{8}$ x $8\frac{1}{2}$.     0-486-42084-1

A SHORT ACCOUNT OF THE HISTORY OF MATHEMATICS, W. W. Rouse Ball. One of clearest, most authoritative surveys from the Egyptians and Phoenicians through 19th-century figures such as Grassman, Galois, Riemann. Fourth edition. 522pp. $5\frac{3}{8}$ x $8\frac{1}{2}$.     0-486-20630-0

THE HISTORY OF THE CALCULUS AND ITS CONCEPTUAL DEVELOPMENT, Carl B. Boyer. Origins in antiquity, medieval contributions, work of Newton, Leibniz, rigorous formulation. Treatment is verbal. 346pp. $5\frac{3}{8}$ x $8\frac{1}{2}$.     0-486-60509-4

THE HISTORICAL ROOTS OF ELEMENTARY MATHEMATICS, Lucas N. H. Bunt, Phillip S. Jones, and Jack D. Bedient. Fundamental underpinnings of modern arithmetic, algebra, geometry and number systems derived from ancient civilizations. 320pp. $5\frac{3}{8}$ x $8\frac{1}{2}$.     0-486-25563-8

THE HISTORY OF THE CALCULUS AND ITS CONCEPTUAL DEVELOPMENT, Carl B. Boyer. Fluent description of the development of both the integral and differential calculus—its early beginnings in antiquity, medieval contributions, and a consideration of Newton and Leibniz. 368pp. $5\frac{3}{8}$ x $8\frac{1}{2}$.     0-486-60509-4

GAMES, GODS & GAMBLING: A HISTORY OF PROBABILITY AND STATISTICAL IDEAS, F. N. David. Episodes from the lives of Galileo, Fermat, Pascal, and others illustrate this fascinating account of the roots of mathematics. Features thought-provoking references to classics, archaeology, biography, poetry. 1962 edition. 304pp. $5\frac{3}{8}$ x $8\frac{1}{2}$. (Available in U.S. only.)     0-486-40023-9

OF MEN AND NUMBERS: THE STORY OF THE GREAT MATHEMATICIANS, Jane Muir. Fascinating accounts of the lives and accomplishments of history's greatest mathematical minds—Pythagoras, Descartes, Euler, Pascal, Cantor, many more. Anecdotal, illuminating. 30 diagrams. Bibliography. 256pp. $5\frac{3}{8}$ x $8\frac{1}{2}$.     0-486-28973-7

HISTORY OF MATHEMATICS, David E. Smith. Nontechnical survey from ancient Greece and Orient to late 19th century; evolution of arithmetic, geometry, trigonometry, calculating devices, algebra, the calculus. 362 illustrations. 1,355pp. $5\frac{3}{8}$ x $8\frac{1}{2}$. Two-vol. set.     Vol. I: 0-486-20429-4     Vol. II: 0-486-20430-8

A CONCISE HISTORY OF MATHEMATICS, Dirk J. Struik. The best brief history of mathematics. Stresses origins and covers every major figure from ancient Near East to 19th century. 41 illustrations. 195pp. $5\frac{3}{8}$ x $8\frac{1}{2}$.     0-486-60255-9

# Physics

OPTICAL RESONANCE AND TWO-LEVEL ATOMS, L. Allen and J. H. Eberly. Clear, comprehensive introduction to basic principles behind all quantum optical resonance phenomena. 53 illustrations. Preface. Index. 256pp. $5\frac{3}{8}$ x $8\frac{1}{2}$.    0-486-65533-4

QUANTUM THEORY, David Bohm. This advanced undergraduate-level text presents the quantum theory in terms of qualitative and imaginative concepts, followed by specific applications worked out in mathematical detail. Preface. Index. 655pp. $5\frac{3}{8}$ x $8\frac{1}{2}$.
0-486-65969-0

ATOMIC PHYSICS (8th EDITION), Max Born. Nobel laureate's lucid treatment of kinetic theory of gases, elementary particles, nuclear atom, wave-corpuscles, atomic structure and spectral lines, much more. Over 40 appendices, bibliography. 495pp. $5\frac{3}{8}$ x $8\frac{1}{2}$.
0-486-65984-4

A SOPHISTICATE'S PRIMER OF RELATIVITY, P. W. Bridgman. Geared toward readers already acquainted with special relativity, this book transcends the view of theory as a working tool to answer natural questions: What is a frame of reference? What is a "law of nature"? What is the role of the "observer"? Extensive treatment, written in terms accessible to those without a scientific background. 1983 ed. xlviii+172pp. $5\frac{3}{8}$ x $8\frac{1}{2}$.
0-486-42549-5

AN INTRODUCTION TO HAMILTONIAN OPTICS, H. A. Buchdahl. Detailed account of the Hamiltonian treatment of aberration theory in geometrical optics. Many classes of optical systems defined in terms of the symmetries they possess. Problems with detailed solutions. 1970 edition. xv + 360pp. $5\frac{3}{8}$ x $8\frac{1}{2}$.    0-486-67597-1

PRIMER OF QUANTUM MECHANICS, Marvin Chester. Introductory text examines the classical quantum bead on a track: its state and representations; operator eigenvalues; harmonic oscillator and bound bead in a symmetric force field; and bead in a spherical shell. Other topics include spin, matrices, and the structure of quantum mechanics; the simplest atom; indistinguishable particles; and stationary-state perturbation theory. 1992 ed. xiv+314pp. $6\frac{1}{8}$ x $9\frac{1}{4}$.    0-486-42878-8

LECTURES ON QUANTUM MECHANICS, Paul A. M. Dirac. Four concise, brilliant lectures on mathematical methods in quantum mechanics from Nobel Prize-winning quantum pioneer build on idea of visualizing quantum theory through the use of classical mechanics. 96pp. $5\frac{3}{8}$ x $8\frac{1}{2}$.    0-486-41713-1

THIRTY YEARS THAT SHOOK PHYSICS: THE STORY OF QUANTUM THEORY, George Gamow. Lucid, accessible introduction to influential theory of energy and matter. Careful explanations of Dirac's anti-particles, Bohr's model of the atom, much more. 12 plates. Numerous drawings. 240pp. $5\frac{3}{8}$ x $8\frac{1}{2}$.    0-486-24895-X

ELECTRONIC STRUCTURE AND THE PROPERTIES OF SOLIDS: THE PHYSICS OF THE CHEMICAL BOND, Walter A. Harrison. Innovative text offers basic understanding of the electronic structure of covalent and ionic solids, simple metals, transition metals and their compounds. Problems. 1980 edition. 582pp. $6\frac{1}{8}$ x $9\frac{1}{4}$.
0-486-66021-4

HYDRODYNAMIC AND HYDROMAGNETIC STABILITY, S. Chandrasekhar. Lucid examination of the Rayleigh-Benard problem; clear coverage of the theory of instabilities causing convection. 704pp. 5⅜ x 8¼. 0-486-64071-X

INVESTIGATIONS ON THE THEORY OF THE BROWNIAN MOVEMENT, Albert Einstein. Five papers (1905–8) investigating dynamics of Brownian motion and evolving elementary theory. Notes by R. Fürth. 122pp. 5⅜ x 8½. 0-486-60304-0

THE PHYSICS OF WAVES, William C. Elmore and Mark A. Heald. Unique overview of classical wave theory. Acoustics, optics, electromagnetic radiation, more. Ideal as classroom text or for self-study. Problems. 477pp. 5⅜ x 8½. 0-486-64926-1

GRAVITY, George Gamow. Distinguished physicist and teacher takes reader-friendly look at three scientists whose work unlocked many of the mysteries behind the laws of physics: Galileo, Newton, and Einstein. Most of the book focuses on Newton's ideas, with a concluding chapter on post-Einsteinian speculations concerning the relationship between gravity and other physical phenomena. 160pp. 5⅜ x 8½. 0-486-42563-0

PHYSICAL PRINCIPLES OF THE QUANTUM THEORY, Werner Heisenberg. Nobel Laureate discusses quantum theory, uncertainty, wave mechanics, work of Dirac, Schroedinger, Compton, Wilson, Einstein, etc. 184pp. 5⅜ x 8½. 0-486-60113-7

ATOMIC SPECTRA AND ATOMIC STRUCTURE, Gerhard Herzberg. One of best introductions; especially for specialist in other fields. Treatment is physical rather than mathematical. 80 illustrations. 257pp. 5⅜ x 8½. 0-486-60115-3

AN INTRODUCTION TO STATISTICAL THERMODYNAMICS, Terrell L. Hill. Excellent basic text offers wide-ranging coverage of quantum statistical mechanics, systems of interacting molecules, quantum statistics, more. 523pp. 5⅜ x 8½. 0-486-65242-4

THEORETICAL PHYSICS, Georg Joos, with Ira M. Freeman. Classic overview covers essential math, mechanics, electromagnetic theory, thermodynamics, quantum mechanics, nuclear physics, other topics. First paperback edition. xxiii + 885pp. 5⅜ x 8½. 0-486-65227-0

PROBLEMS AND SOLUTIONS IN QUANTUM CHEMISTRY AND PHYSICS, Charles S. Johnson, Jr. and Lee G. Pedersen. Unusually varied problems, detailed solutions in coverage of quantum mechanics, wave mechanics, angular momentum, molecular spectroscopy, more. 280 problems plus 139 supplementary exercises. 430pp. 6½ x 9¼. 0-486-65236-X

THEORETICAL SOLID STATE PHYSICS, Vol. 1: Perfect Lattices in Equilibrium; Vol. II: Non-Equilibrium and Disorder, William Jones and Norman H. March. Monumental reference work covers fundamental theory of equilibrium properties of perfect crystalline solids, non-equilibrium properties, defects and disordered systems. Appendices. Problems. Preface. Diagrams. Index. Bibliography. Total of 1,301pp. 5⅜ x 8½. Two volumes. Vol. I: 0-486-65015-4 Vol. II: 0-486-65016-2

WHAT IS RELATIVITY? L. D. Landau and G. B. Rumer. Written by a Nobel Prize physicist and his distinguished colleague, this compelling book explains the special theory of relativity to readers with no scientific background, using such familiar objects as trains, rulers, and clocks. 1960 ed. vi+72pp. 5⅜ x 8½. 0-486-42806-0

*CATALOG OF DOVER BOOKS*

A TREATISE ON ELECTRICITY AND MAGNETISM, James Clerk Maxwell. Important foundation work of modern physics. Brings to final form Maxwell's theory of electromagnetism and rigorously derives his general equations of field theory. 1,084pp. $5\frac{3}{8} \times 8\frac{1}{2}$. Two-vol. set. Vol. I: 0-486-60636-8 Vol. II: 0-486-60637-6

MATHEMATICS FOR PHYSICISTS, Philippe Dennery and Andre Krzywicki. Superb text provides math needed to understand today's more advanced topics in physics and engineering. Theory of functions of a complex variable, linear vector spaces, much more. Problems. 1967 edition. 400pp. $6\frac{1}{2} \times 9\frac{1}{4}$. 0-486-69193-4

INTRODUCTION TO QUANTUM MECHANICS WITH APPLICATIONS TO CHEMISTRY, Linus Pauling & E. Bright Wilson, Jr. Classic undergraduate text by Nobel Prize winner applies quantum mechanics to chemical and physical problems. Numerous tables and figures enhance the text. Chapter bibliographies. Appendices. Index. 468pp. $5\frac{3}{8} \times 8\frac{1}{2}$. 0-486-64871-0

METHODS OF THERMODYNAMICS, Howard Reiss. Outstanding text focuses on physical technique of thermodynamics, typical problem areas of understanding, and significance and use of thermodynamic potential. 1965 edition. 238pp. $5\frac{3}{8} \times 8\frac{1}{2}$. 0-486-69445-3

THE ELECTROMAGNETIC FIELD, Albert Shadowitz. Comprehensive under- graduate text covers basics of electric and magnetic fields, builds up to electromagnetic theory. Also related topics, including relativity. Over 900 problems. 768pp. $5\frac{5}{8} \times 8\frac{1}{4}$. 0-486-65660-8

GREAT EXPERIMENTS IN PHYSICS: FIRSTHAND ACCOUNTS FROM GALILEO TO EINSTEIN, Morris H. Shamos (ed.). 25 crucial discoveries: Newton's laws of motion, Chadwick's study of the neutron, Hertz on electromagnetic waves, more. Original accounts clearly annotated. 370pp. $5\frac{3}{8} \times 8\frac{1}{2}$. 0-486-25346-5

EINSTEIN'S LEGACY, Julian Schwinger. A Nobel Laureate relates fascinating story of Einstein and development of relativity theory in well-illustrated, nontechnical volume. Subjects include meaning of time, paradoxes of space travel, gravity and its effect on light, non-Euclidean geometry and curving of space-time, impact of radio astronomy and space-age discoveries, and more. 189 b/w illustrations. xiv+250pp. $8\frac{3}{8} \times 9\frac{1}{4}$. 0-486-41974-6

THE VARIATIONAL PRINCIPLES OF MECHANICS, Cornelius Lanczos. Philosophic, less formalistic approach to analytical mechanics offers model of clear, scholarly exposition at graduate level with coverage of basics, calculus of variations, principle of virtual work, equations of motion, more. 418pp. $5\frac{3}{8} \times 8\frac{1}{2}$. 0-486-65067-7

Paperbound unless otherwise indicated. Available at your book dealer, online at www.doverpublications.com, or by writing to Dept. GI, Dover Publications, Inc., 31 East 2nd Street, Mineola, NY 11501. For current price information or for free catalogues (please indicate field of interest), write to Dover Publications or log on to www.doverpublications.com and see every Dover book in print. Dover publishes more than 400 books each year on science, elementary and advanced mathematics, biology, music, art, literary history, social sciences, and other areas.